**New Directions for
Teaching and Learning**

Marilla D. Svinicki
Catherine M. Wehlburg
CO-EDITORS-IN-CHIEF

As the Spirit Moves Us:
Embracing Spirituality in the Postsecondary Experience

Katherine Grace Hendrix
Janice D. Hamlet
EDITORS

Number 120 • Winter 2009
Jossey-Bass
San Francisco

As the Spirit Moves Us: Embracing Spirituality in the
Postsecondary Experience
Katherine Grace Hendrix, Janice D. Hamlet (eds.)
New Directions for Teaching and Learning, no. 120
Marilla D. Svinicki, Catherine M. Wehlburg, Co-Editors-in-Chief

Microfilm copies of issues and articles are available in 16mm and 35mm,
as well as microfiche in 105mm, through University Microfilms, Inc.,
300 North Zeeb Road, Ann Arbor, MI 48106-1346.

NEW DIRECTIONS FOR TEACHING AND LEARNING (ISSN 0271-0633, elec-
tronic ISSN 1536-0768) is part of The Jossey-Bass Higher and Adult
Education Series and is published quarterly by Wiley Subscription Ser-
vices, Inc., A Wiley Company, at Jossey-Bass, 989 Market Street, San
Francisco, CA 94103-1741. Periodicals postage paid at San Francisco,
CA, and at additional mailing offices. POSTMASTER: Send address
changes to New Directions for Teaching and Learning, Jossey-Bass, 989
Market Street, San Francisco, CA 94103-1741.

New Directions for Teaching and Learning is indexed in CIJE: Current
Index to Journals in Education (ERIC), Contents Pages in Education
(T&F), Current Abstracts (EBSCO), Educational Research Abstracts
Online (T&F), ERIC Database (Education Resources Information Cen-
ter), Higher Education Abstracts (Claremont Graduate University), and
SCOPUS (Elsevier).

SUBSCRIPTIONS cost $98 for individuals and $267 for institutions, agencies,
and libraries in the United States. Prices subject to change.

EDITORIAL CORRESPONDENCE should be sent to the co-editor-in-chief,
Marilla D. Svinicki, Department of Educational Psychology, University of
Texas at Austin, One University Station, D5800, Austin, TX 78712.

www.josseybass.com

CONTENTS

FROM THE SERIES EDITORS

About This Publication

Since 1980, *New Directions for Teaching and Learning* has brought a unique blend of theory, research, and practice to leaders in postsecondary education. NDTL sourcebooks strive not only for solid substance but also for timeliness, compactness, and accessibility.

The series has four goals: to inform readers about current and future directions in teaching and learning in postsecondary education, to illuminate the context that shapes these new directions, to illustrate these new directions through examples from real settings, and to propose ways in which these new directions can be incorporated into still other settings.

This publication reflects the view that teaching deserves respect as a high form of scholarship. We believe that significant scholarship is conducted not only by researchers who report results of empirical investigation but also by practitioners who share disciplinary reflection about teaching. Contributors to *NDTL* approach questions of teaching and learning as seriously as they approach substantive questions in their own disciplines, and they deal with pedagogical issues and also the intellectual and social context in which these issues arise. Authors deal on the one hand with theory and research and on the other with practice, and they translate from research and theory to practice and back again.

About This Volume

Spirituality can have an impact on how one approaches education and can influence choices in pedagogy, reflection, and style of communication. This issue of *NDTL* explores how individual spirituality influences can affect interactions with students and colleagues.

Marilla D. Svinicki
Catherine M. Wehlburg
Co-Editors-in-Chief

MARILLA D. SVINICKI is the director of the Center for Teaching Effectiveness at the University of Texas at Austin.

CATHERINE M. WEHLBURG is the Assistant Provost for Institutional Effectiveness at Texas Christian University.

SECTION ONE

Spirituality as a Way of Being in the World

1

How can one embrace spirituality in the workplace? This volume provides varied responses to this question through autoethnographic narratives from a racially diverse and spiritually guided group of professors and administrators.

Introduction: Our Way of Being in the World

Katherine Grace Hendrix, Janice D. Hamlet

As the Spirit Moves Us: Embracing Spirituality in the Postsecondary Experience chronicles the experiences of a racially diverse group of Christian professors of communication, focusing on their experiences within higher education, in order to promote an increased understanding of (1) the intrapersonal reflection and outlook of a spiritually guided professor/administrator, (2) classroom pedagogy of such individuals, (3) interpersonal relationships between such professors and their students, (4) the coping mechanisms emanating from a spiritual grounding, and (5) the power of the reflective voice captured through autoethnography. Hence, these contributors offer nine vantage points from which to understand how spirituality influences our interactions with students and professional colleagues.

As editors, this project grew out of our need to address the topic of spirituality from a more traditional orientation, one with which we were familiar and of which we could acknowledge the usefulness. The impetus for this volume came as a result of our being in the audience of several communication conference panels where presenters discussed spirituality in unconventional, and to some extent shocking, ways. Listening to papers focusing on spirituality as expressing one's sexuality, spirituality as ecology, and even spirituality as related to female menstrual and menopausal stages had us bewildered and wondering whatever happened to the idea of spirituality as feeling the presence of a higher power and tapping into that power.

Because we did not hear presentations of the latter sort and could not relate to the ones we did hear, we decided to create a venue to allow our

NEW DIRECTIONS FOR TEACHING AND LEARNING, no. 120, Winter 2009   © Wiley Periodicals, Inc.
Published online in Wiley InterScience (www.interscience.wiley.com) • DOI: 10.1002/tl.371

testimonies and the testimonies of likeminded colleagues bearing witness to a higher power. To create a space for more traditional voices, we intentionally draw on the power that emanates from sharing one's lived experience as noted by prominent qualitative scholars (see Ellis and Bochner, 2000; Conquergood, 1991; Goodall, 2000; Lincoln and Denzin, 2003; Reed-Danahay, 1997; Trujillo, 2004). As a result, *As the Spirit Moves Us* privileges spirituality as the presence of a higher power, and autoethnography, rather than theory or empirical research, as a legitimate way of obtaining knowledge—and ultimately understanding our experiences.

Spirituality

As popular as the subject of spirituality has become, its meanings and interpretations are varied, complex, and often perplexing. Some scholars disconnect spirituality from religion while offering a definition tied to everything from an internal compass to community to powers emanating from ecological resources. In an effort to address the complexities of what spirituality means, Pokora (2001) designed a typology that groups the various meanings of spirituality into four categories: linking spirituality, path spirituality, incorporeal spirituality, and totalizing spirituality. *Linking spirituality* is manifested by a person who has a belief in God or some kind of higher power and puts her or his faith into action. *Path spirituality* offers specific practices designed to help one experience or develop a closer relationship with the Divine; meditation techniques, fasting, prayers are examples of path spirituality. *Incorporeal spirituality* can be understood as that which is separate from matter. Spirituality, then, is the quality or fact of being spiritual. This is the basic understanding of spirituality commonly found in dictionaries. Finally, *totalizing spirituality* reflects the belief that everything is spirituality, including the material. Because spirituality pervades our beings, it cannot be separated from our actions, thoughts, or ourselves. Therefore, according to Pokora (2001), spirituality affects and is affected by every other aspect of our lives.

In 1986, Bowen and Schuster described the condition of faculty in the United States as dispirited, fragmented, devalued, and dedicated. These scholars titled their introductory chapter "A National Resource Imperiled," where they stated:

> The academic profession stands at a crossroads. Our colleges and universities and society at large are faced with critical choices that must be made in the next few years. These decisions can lead toward a revitalized faculty fully capable of meeting its considerable responsibilities, or to neglect and perhaps irreparable damage to the nation [p. 8].

Given this discouraging backdrop, it is not surprising to find scholars searching for means to improve the environment in academia for students, faculty, staff, and administrators. Embracing spirituality has been offered as a viable means for restoring energy and promoting new vigor within academic circles.

As spirituality relates to communication, Kirkwood (1994) stresses the importance of studying both communication about spirituality and the spiritual consequences of communication. Witmer (2001) argues that people are imbued with incorporeal spirituality that is also totalizing because spiritual human actors discursively enact it throughout organizational life. Thus, from a communication perspective, spirituality and communication are intimately linked, guided by the premise that humans are spiritual beings engaged in human activities.

The contributors of this volume have all written about their spirituality and workplace experiences from one or more of Pokora's four typologies (2001) as well as an understanding of the scholarship on spirituality we have unearthed. Collectively, however, for us spirituality emerges as a way of being in the world that incorporates beliefs, values, attitudes, emotions, behaviors, and insights, and that informs and may be informed by our lived experiences in our efforts to contribute to our students' transformation (and our own) in discovering our better selves.

Autoethnography

Autoethnography is a genre of writing and research that connects the personal to the cultural, placing the self within a social context (Reed-Danahay, 1997). These texts are usually written in the first person and feature dialogue, emotion, and self-consciousness as relational as well as institutional stories affected by history, social structure, and culture (Ellis and Bochner, 2000). Reed-Danahay explains that autoethnographers may vary in their emphasis on *graphy*, meaning the research process, (*ethno*) culture, or self (*auto*). Whatever the specific focus, authors use their own experiences in a culture to understand the interactions in that culture. These self-reflexive critiques on one's positionality as researcher serve to inspire readers to reflect critically on their own life experiences, constructions of self, and interactions with others within particular sociohistorical contexts (Ellis and Bochner, 1996; Goodall, 1998). Ellis and Bochner (2000) advocate autoethnography as a form of writing that "makes the researcher's own experience a topic of investigation in its own right rather than seeming as if they're written from nowhere by nobody" (p. 734). Autoethnographers ask their readers to feel the truth of their stories and to become co-participants, thereby engaging the storyline morally, emotionally, aesthetically, and intellectually.

The emergence of autoethnography as a method of inquiry moves a researcher's use of self-introspection or self-ethnography as a legitimate focus of study in and of itself (Ellis, 1991). The autoethnographic text emerges from the researcher's bodily standpoint, as the scholar continuously recognizes and interprets the residual traces of culture inscribed upon his or her hide from interacting with others in certain contexts. This corporeally textual orientation rejects the notion that lived experiences can be represented only indirectly, through quotations from field notes, observations, or interviews (Denzin, 1992). In autographical methods, the researcher is the epistemological and ontological nexus on which the research process turns (Spry, 2001). Autoethnography and narratives of self are part of this move toward finding new ways to represent our research endeavors.

As such, autoethnography has become increasingly popular in communication research (see Allen, Orbe, and Olivas 1999; Ashton and Denton, 2006; Gonzalez, Houston, and Chen, 2004; Hendrix, 2001; Payne, 1996), education (Tierney and Lincoln, 1997), and other disciplines including sociology (Atkinson, Coffey, and Delamont, 2003; Brusma, 2007). As a qualitative research method, it has an interpretive character whose purpose is to discover the meanings that events and experiences have not only for the individual who experiences them but also for readers who may have had similar experiences and struggled for interpretation and meaning.

Organization of the Volume

The chapters in this volume tend to fall into one of three general themes: spirituality as a way of being in the world, spirituality as self-discovery and insight, or spirituality as discovering the strength to endure. We believe that an understanding of communication that rests on spirituality, as we have defined it, broadens our appreciation of such and in so doing broadens our knowledge of what being human means. In our stories, we explore the challenges in our workplace lives, and we present spiritual practices that have helped us to not only survive but thrive.

References

Allen, B. M. Orbe, and Olivas, M. R. "The Complexity of Our Tears: Disenchantment and (in) Difference in the Academy." *Communication Theory*, 1999, *9*, 402–429.

Ashton, W., and Denton, D. (eds.). *Spirituality, Ethnography, and Teaching: Stories from Within.* New York: Peter Lang, 2006.

Atkinson, P., Coffey, A., and Delamont, S. *Key Themes in Qualitative Research: Continuities and Changes.* Walnut Creek, Calif.: AltaMira Press, 2003.

Bowen, H. R., and Schuster, J. H. *American Professors: A National Resource Imperiled.* Fairlawn, N.J.: Oxford University Press, 1986.

Brusma, D. L. "White Lives as Covert Racism." In R. D. Coates (ed.), *Covert Racism.* New York: Oxford Press, 2007.

Conquergood, D. "Rethinking Ethnography: Towards a Critical Cultural Politics." *Communication Monographs*, 1991, *58*, 179–194.

Denzin, N. K. "The Many Faces of Emotionality." In C. Ellis (ed.), *Investigating Subjectivity: Research on Lived Experience.* London: Sage, 1992.

Ellis, C. "Sociological Introspection and Emotional Experience." *Symbolic Interaction*, 1991, *14*, 23–50.

Ellis, C., and Bochner, A. P. *Composing Ethnography: Alternative Forms of Qualitative Writing.* Walnut Creek, Calif.: AltaMira Press, 1996.

Ellis, C., and Bochner, A. "Autoethnography, Personal Narrative, Reflexivity: Researcher as Subject." In N. K. Denzin and Y. S. Lincoln (eds.), *Handbook of Qualitative Research* (2nd ed.). Thousand Oaks, Calif.: Sage, 2000.

Gonzalez, A., Houston. M., and Chen, V. (eds.) *Our Voices: Essays in Culture, Ethnicity, and Communication* (4th ed.). Los Angeles: Roxbury Press, 2004.

Goodall, H. L. Notes for the autoethnography and autobiography panel NCA. Paper presented at meeting of National Communication Association, November 1998, New York.

Goodall, H. L. *Writing the New Ethnography.* Walnut Creek, Calif.: AltaMira Press, 2000.

Hendrix, K. G. "Mama Told Me . . . : Exploring How Childhood Lessons Laid a Foundation for My 'Endarkened' Epistemology." *Qualitative Inquiry*, 2001, 7, 559–577.

Kirkwood, W. G. "Studying Communication About Spirituality and the Spiritual Consequences of Communication." *Journal of Communication and Religion*, 1994, 17(1), 13–26.

Lincoln, Y. S., and Denzin, N. (eds.). *Turning Points in Qualitative Research: Tying Knots in a Handkerchief.* Walnut Creek, Calif.: AltaMira Press, 2003.

Payne, D. "Autobiology." In C. Ellis and A. P. Bochner (eds.), *Composing Ethnography: Alternative Forms of Qualitative Writing.* Walnut Creek, Calif.: AltaMira Press, 1996.

Pokora, R. M. "Implications of Conceptualizations of Spirituality for Organizational Communication." In A. Rodriquez (ed.), *Essays on Communication & Spirituality: Contributions to a New Discourse on Communication.* Lanham, N.Y.: University Press of America, 2001.

Reed-Danahay, D. (ed.). *Auto/Ethnography: Rewriting the Self and the Social.* Oxford, UK: Berg, 1997.

Spry, T. "Performing Autoethnography: An Embodied Methodological Praxis." *Qualitative Inquiry*, 2001, 7, 706–732.

Tierney, W. G., and Lincoln, Y. S. *Representation and the Text Reframing the Narrative Voice.* Albany: SUNY Press, 1997.

Trujillo, N. *In Search of Naunny's Grave: Age, Class, Gender, and Ethnicity in an American Family.* Walnut Creek, Calif.: AltaMira Press, 2004.

Witmer, D. F. "The Co-Construction of Self and Organization: Evoking Organizational Spirituality." In A. Rodriquez (ed.), *Essays on Communication & Spirituality: Contributions to a New Discourse on Communication.* Lanham, N.Y.: University Press of America, 2001.

KATHERINE GRACE HENDRIX *is an associate professor in the Communication Department at the University of Memphis. She is an instructional communication scholar dedicated to the scholarship of teaching, with a particular interest in the pedagogical contributions of and credibility challenges faced by professors and graduate teaching assistants of color. She has published in numerous journals and edited books.*

JANICE D. HAMLET *is an associate professor of communication at Northern Illinois University in Dekalb, Illinois. Her research interests focus on African American culture and rhetoric, womanist epistemology and theology, rhetorical theory and criticism, and culture and pedagogy. She has edited two books and published in numerous journals and edited books.*

2

This autoethnographic account describes interconnections among a professor's personal prayer life, teaching, and research. The contextual frame for the story includes episodes and observations from a twelve-year span, encompassing postacademic tenure and promotion to the present.

Prayer Life of a Professor

E. James Baesler

I close my eyes in prayer and images from the past appear like gifts from the sea of time, deposited briefly on the foamy shores of this present moment, then slipping back into the seabed of consciousness . . . images of bedtime prayers ("Now I lay me down to sleep"), and praying before first communion (I see the gold chalice and white host emblazed on the front cover of my black prayer book, a small chapel, friends and family gathered, words spoken as a prayer to my one true love: "To love, honor and cherish"). These are some of the gifts from the seabed of consciousness belonging to a Catholic religious/spiritual heritage that frames and influences my prayer life as a professor. I punctuate this particular story with the period immediately following tenure and promotion to the present, focusing on how my personal prayer life has influenced my teaching and research. My prayer is that others might resonate with parts of this story and discover and explore how prayer can spiritually nourish their teaching and research.

Methodological Assumptions

Two methodologies influence how I tell this story. First, I borrow from Coles's story-telling tradition (1990), which presumes that (1) we have awareness and consciousness, (2) it is through language that we understand the world and can communicate what we learn to others, (3) conclusions and generalizations are less important than the veracity of phenomenological descriptions of lived experience, and (4) the best way to learn is through "prolonged encounters" with others where we let others tell their story. Second, the autoethnographic approach of Goodall (1996) provides many

insights that inform the present story, among them that (1) spiritual meaning is found in community by analyzing the nexus of private and public messages; (2) imagination engages the map of "what is" to envision spiritual possibilities of "what can be"; (3) spiritual autoethnography uses everyday signs as openings to the spiritual interconnectedness of all life, that is, anything can become a trigger for spiritual messages having multiple interpretations, levels, contexts, and perspectives; (4) paying attention to details is essential because they contain the whole story; and finally (5) stories are meant to be connected to other stories, to be part of a dialogue, a sharing of spirits.

Demarcation: Post Tenure and Spiritual Renewal

Is there life after tenure and promotion from assistant professor to associate professor? Relief and confusion accompanied news of tenure and promotion—relief from proving competencies in teaching, research, and service, and confusion about the import and meaning of my research agenda. Relief and confusion soon gave way to God's grace and the stirrings of a spiritual awakening. The security of tenure and promotion unleashed new feelings and intuitions from their interior home in the seabed of consciousness. The feelings bubble, like the effervescence of newly opened champagne, but instead of lessening in intensity over time they grew in frequency and intensity, culminating in a time of spiritual renewal at the Well Retreat Center situated in the Isle of Wright County in Virginia, a place bounded by tall maples, pines, and a small lake, teeming with a variety of wildlife.

During the first of what would be nearly thirty silent retreats spaced over the course of the next decade at the Well Retreat Center, I felt free from academic and family concerns. I basked in the beauty of nature, ate simply, breathed deeply. It wasn't long before I discovered the center's library filled with books and tapes on spiritual topics. Somewhere in the early morning hours after midnight, I found a series of audiotapes on prayer by Trappist monk William Meninger (n.d.). He narrates a story about an immigrant family spending everything they had to purchase tickets to America by ship, saving their last crusts of bread and cheese for the long journey. On about the third day of the voyage, the eldest son, after completing his exploration of the ship, returns to the family with unbelievable news about the most delicious pies, meats, and fruit. The father thinks the lad is delusional but follows him anyway to a dining hall where they discover a banquet. It seems that the price of the ticket included the meals. All they had to do was show their ticket, enter the hall, and enjoy the feast! So it is with prayer, says Meninger. Most of us have become accustomed to eating stale bread and cheese, and we do not realize that we possess a ticket to a heavenly banquet that we can begin enjoying right now. I desperately wanted to taste this "prayer banquet," so I put Meninger's advice on prayer to the test by devoting regular time to the practice of contemplative prayer. The spiritual discipline of contemplative prayer has since touched every aspect of my life,

NEW DIRECTIONS FOR TEACHING AND LEARNING • DOI: 10.1002/tl

including my life of teaching and research as a professor. Contemplative prayer remains a significant portion of my daily existence, as easy to do as brushing my teeth, as comfortable as an old friend, and imbued with the fullness of spiritual meaning and life.

From Personal to Professional Prayer Passions

Prayer and Research. The first major academic decision I made as a result of my experiences at the Well Retreat Center was to radically change the direction of my research. I felt called to expand and deepen my personal prayer life, and to conduct scholarly research on prayer. I still faced the reality of producing research for yearly faculty evaluations, but I no longer wanted to simply publish to build a thicker vitae. I wanted to publish research related to prayer, galvanizing other scholars in the pursuit of prayer research, and contributing to the vitality of spiritual lives.

Praying for direction and wisdom, like some prophets of the Hebrew Scriptures, I struck a deal with God:

> If You really want me to do this prayer research, You're going to have to help me. I don't know anything about conducting "prayer research." All I have is this desire to serve You, this sense that You're calling me to this work of prayer. I need Your guidance and support, and I need "signs" along the way that I'm in Your will. *If* You bless this work with talks, workshops, convention papers, and publications in journals, *then* I'll continue to work, but if You decide I need to do something different, then I'll close up shop, and follow wherever You lead.

After more than a decade of prayer research, God is still answering my heartfelt prayer, guiding and supporting the work of prayer with talks, workshops, convention papers, journal articles, and a scholarly book.

The prayer research journey hasn't been without anxiety and doubts. I had no idea what to do for successive projects until, nearing completion of the current project, I would see that God provided only enough inspiration and direction to begin the next project. In hindsight, the actual program of research appears quite logical, even planned, but the enactment of projects was an amalgam of prayer, intuition, and serendipity. For example, consider the serendipitous nature of one episode. One summer I found myself in the library stacks searching for a reference, when I saw a faculty member in psychology whom I had met only a few times before. He recognized me and inquired about my research. I narrated my story about prayer research and he said (paraphrased), "Curious you should mention prayer. I have this dataset of interviews with mothers with HIV, and even though I didn't ask them, they spontaneously talked about their relationship with God and their prayer lives. I have no idea what to do with these data. What do you think?" Several collaborative conversations and sessions later, we coauthored an article on prayer and mothers with HIV (Baesler, Derlega,

Winstead, and Barbee, 2003). This kind of serendipitous encounter is not coincidence for me, but part of God's plan for a prayer research agenda.

Only in the last year has God offered more guidance for what kinds of prayer research are possible, and as with the prophet John the Baptist in the opening of the Christian gospel of Mark, I feel like a voice in the wilderness, a herald of sorts, envisioning a new research agenda housed in an interdisciplinary prayer institute, where a critical mass of scholars engage in collaborative programs of funded prayer research. Over time, hundreds of prayer projects have emerged from the Spirit's seabed of consciousness. I have at least fifty of these projects in various stages of completion written on a "scroll" (a huge piece of drafting paper). I've prayed for nearly a decade to meet other scholars, and over time a handful of collaborative relationships developed.

I still pray for direction, discernment, support, and wisdom in creating and conducting prayer research, especially at the beginnings and ends of each semester, but also week to week during the term. Prayerful meditation on research questions can be part of *any* professor's research agenda: Am I on track with God's will for this particular project? Are there needs in the community related to my research that I should be addressing? Am I trying to do too much alone? Have I discerned the appropriate priorities among the several research projects? These questions are worth praying over again and again; doing so renders fresh ideas for the research journey every time.

Prayer and Teaching. Prayer talks. Ideally, prayer research influences content of teaching. I began giving talks on prayer at my local church for those entering the church through rites of Christian initiation, and for those participating in various types of adult religious formation. In both cases, the outcomes of the prayer talks were similar. Audiences seemed interested and curious, had questions, and made comments afterwards such as "very interesting" and "I really liked your presentation," but coordinators of the talks did not invite me to speak again on prayer. Similar reactions over the years came from audiences of different sizes and ages and in a variety of venues. Why were responses to these prayer talks uniformly generic and positive, and why was I not invited to speak again? I still don't know the answers to these questions, and the most troublesome unanswered question that bothers me is, Did the prayer talks have any impact on the listener's prayer life? Without systematic evaluation and assessment, there is no scientific way to answer this question. I have approached some of these groups with ideas for assessment, but the answer is usually some version of "We don't have the time for that," "We cannot commit to that," "We have enough to do as it is," and so forth. Then why continue the prayer talks? I have faith that in a small way the prayer talks make a difference to some people. Hence my policy on prayer talks is the same as it was over a decade ago: I do not seek to speak about prayer; rather I wait to be invited, and if in praying about the invitation I feel God calling me to speak, I do so.

New Directions for Teaching and Learning • DOI: 10.1002/tl

Developing Prayer Courses. Talking about prayer for an hour or two to an audience that I'm not likely to meet again is a different teaching environment from lecturing for three hours a week to a large class for an entire academic term. I was somewhat embarrassed recently when visiting with a collaborator for a prayer project at another local university when he discovered that I didn't teach any academic courses on prayer. "You mean you don't teach in your primary research specialty?!" I then described the prayer talks I had been giving, and the fate of my attempts to teach an academic course on prayer.

I felt called to develop an academic course on prayer about six years ago. As an initial step, I searched 309 Christian college Web sites for academic course offerings on prayer. Finding seventeen academic prayer courses, I persuaded seven instructors to share their syllabi with me. Content analyses of these syllabi, along with what I had been learning about prayer during the past several years, constituted the basis for developing a detailed academic course syllabus on prayer (for the complete syllabus and details of the method, see Baesler, 2000). With this research background complete, I felt ready to offer a course on prayer and presented the idea to a local private Christian college. They were receptive to the idea and we listed the first "Communication and Prayer" course as a summer offering for their graduate program in communication, but the course was not offered because of "insufficient enrollment." I was disappointed and let another year pass before sensing a call to teach an academic course on prayer. I revised the Communication and Prayer syllabus to reach a broader audience, entitling the course "Religious Communication" and targeting it to graduate students in the Master's in Humanities Program. The course was offered in the evening during the regular semester, but it too suffered from insufficient enrollment.

Only last year did God resurrect the call to teach an academic course on prayer. Some of our faculty were considering developing a master's degree in communication, health, and wellness and suggested we develop undergraduate topic courses in our primary research areas to be later revised and offered as part of the graduate program. The course is scheduled to be offered next fall. Only God knows if this course will meet the same demise as the previous two prayer courses for insufficient enrollment, but I feel hopeful and have a sense that this may be my debut of teaching prayer in the academy. In hindsight, it seems that God's timing is not necessarily my timing. The apparent failures of previous prayer courses gave me more time to grow in my personal and professional understanding of prayer, and this contributed to revisions in the current course offering on prayer. I'm beginning to learn that, despite multiple setbacks, I need to continually open myself to the possibility that God fosters opportunities to teach in the area of my research specialty. Overall, my prayer research has only partially translated into content for teaching prayer, but prayer has influenced the teaching of my regular academic courses in other significant ways.

NEW DIRECTIONS FOR TEACHING AND LEARNING • DOI: 10.1002/tl

Personal Prayer and Teaching Regular Courses. My personal prayer life has become part of my academic teaching without much conscious awareness of the application and translation process. For example, after teaching college courses for twenty some years, I still found myself getting terribly nervous before the first day of classes—nightmares, feeling ill and sick to my stomach, doubting my ability to teach effectively. All that changed one semester after morning prayer as I gazed over a roster of students I would soon meet for the first time. Still feeling in the contemplative space following morning prayer, I began slowly reciting the names of the students, growing in the realization that these names represent eternal spiritual beings, and that we in the forthcoming semester would shape our eternal destiny together. I began praying for them, a simple prayer that God would bless them. Somewhere during this blessing prayer, anxiety began to melt, replaced by a sense of peace, knowing that a spiritual kinship was initiated. I began anticipating the delightful union of name and face that soon would take place, rejoicing in the spiritual connection that had already begun and would continue to grow during the course of the term. Since that time, I've continued the practice of blessing my students before the start of each term. It not only relieves most of the preterm apprehension but more importantly opens a spiritual dimension to the student-teacher relationship. I begin to see deeper levels of our relationship, levels that foster growth, encouragement, inspiration, kindness, hope—things representing the eternal manifestation of the Spirit, things that will last for eternity.

My personal prayer life has influenced the teaching of regular course offerings in other profound ways. Cultivating a contemplative prayer life changes one from the inside out. One of these spiritual transformations is a growing attitude of receptiveness to life, including the lives of my hundred some students each semester. The spiritual discipline of cultivating a center within, a place that allows the Spirit entry to work and move, spills over into my personal relationships, including my relationships with students. I find myself less defensive, more ready to openly admit my errors (even laugh at them), a greater willingness to be vulnerable when listening, a conscious effort to engage in authentic dialogue (Swidler, 1999). Contemplative prayer has helped me become a better listener, focusing on student concerns, worries, challenges, and questions.

Authentic listening can also create a good deal of stress for the listener (Pennebaker, 1990); hence over time I've discovered some practical prayer strategies to cope with the stress of being a professor. First, I allot part of my lunch hour for personal prayer in a private place. In the midst of a busy day, prayer can shed much of the unwanted stress that accumulates from little stressors such as unexpected traffic commuting to work; an unkind word or look; minor conflicts before, during, or after class. Prayer during midday often slowly dissolves these minor stresses so that I can begin afresh, renewed and energized for the second half of the day.

The second prayer strategy I use to cope with stress is the time-honored tradition of praying the Holy Name (Baesler, 2001). Variations of this prayer occur in most of the major world religions, including Buddhism, Christianity, Hinduism, Islam, Judaism, and Taoism (Benson, 1975). Repetition of the Holy Name is especially useful for coping with negatively charged emotions, not simply repressing negative emotions but spiritually transforming them into a form that can be positively redirected (Easwaran, 1998). In teaching, I might use this prayer strategy when anxious before a lecture, when confronted with a particularly challenging question, or when disappointed or angry with a student's juvenile behavior. Repetition of the Holy Name is a soothing balm for the negative stresses of teaching (and research), and it is also a source of creative inspiration when I need ideas for a lesson plan or just the right phrase for research writing. The process for using this prayer strategy for creative inspiration is described in detail by Benson (1987). From personal experience, I can testify that using the Holy Name to creatively address a challenge doesn't always work the way I anticipate, but I have yet to be disappointed in the end results after several attempts.

Return to the Seabed of Consciousness

I close my eyes, and images from the seabed of consciousness come forth again, old images having new meanings now. I still pray at day's end, no longer as a child: "Thank you God for the gift of life, for these blessings, forgive me for times I fell short, help me serve my students as teacher and discern and engage in research that will benefit others." I still see the host and chalice on Sunday at mass, continuing to receive spiritual nourishment from communion, but now I experience the process of being transformed into bread and drink for others in the ministries of teaching and research. Finally, I still keep my vows of loving, honoring, and cherishing my wife (and two sons), but now the circle of love grows wider, engulfing neighbors, students, colleagues, and beyond. In this seabed of consciousness, I am sustained by the prayer of St. Chrysostom: "Prayer is an all-efficient panoply, a treasure undiminished, a mine that is never exhausted, a sky unobscured by clouds, a heaven unruffled by the storm. It is the root, the fountain, *the mother of a thousand blessings*" (cited in Bounds, 1997, p. 34; emphasis mine).

It is my prayer that all faculty may know and experience the truth of this spiritual message in their teaching, research, and relationships with others.

References

Baesler, E. J. (2000). *Teaching prayer: Pilot survey of academic courses on personal prayer.* ERIC Document (ED44842).

Baesler, E. J. (2001). The prayer of the Holy Name in eastern and western spiritual traditions. *Journal of Ecumenical Studies, 38,* 196–216.

Baesler, E. J. (2003). *Theoretical explorations and empirical investigations of communication and prayer.* Lewiston, NY: Edwin Mellen Press.

Baesler, E. J., Derlega, V. J., Winstead, B. A., & Barbee, A. (2003). Prayer as interpersonal coping in the lives of mothers with HIV. *Women and Therapy, 26,* 283–295.

Benson, H. (1975). *The relaxation response*. NY: William Morrow and Company.

Benson, H. (1987). *Your maximum mind*. NY: Random House.

Bounds, E. (1997). *On prayer*. New Kensington, PA: Whitaker House.

Coles, R. (1990). *The spiritual life of children*. Boston: Houghton Mifflin.

Easwaran, E. (1998). *The mantram handbook* (4th ed.). Tomales, CA: Nilgiri.

Goodall, H. L., Jr. (1996). *Divine signs: Connecting spirit to community*. Carbondale, IL: Southern Illinois University Press.

Meninger, W. (n.d.). *Contemplative prayer* (audio tapes). Spencer, MS: St. Joseph's Cistercian Abbey.

Pennebaker, J. (1990). *Opening up*. NY: Guilford Press.

Swidler, L. (1999). *Seven stages of deep-dialogue*. Global Dialogue Institute. Retrieved May 3, 2007, from http://astro.temple.edu/~dialogue.

E. JAMES BAESLER *is associate professor of communication at Old Dominion University's Department of Communication in Norfolk, Virginia. Baesler has investigated prayer as religious or spiritual communication for more than a decade, publishing several academic articles on the topic in addition to a scholarly book.*

NEW DIRECTIONS FOR TEACHING AND LEARNING • DOI: 10.1002/tl

3

In this chapter the author explains how spiritual mentoring is the everyday enactment of spiritual values into concrete instructional practices. It takes place in several ways: offering opportunities for student development, engaging in spontaneous mentoring, enlarging and enriching resources, and encouraging continuous self-development.

Spiritual Mentoring: Embracing the Mentor-Mentee Relational Process

Patrice M. Buzzanell

I have been blessed to be able to work with a number of students over the years with whom I feel very fortunate to engage because we grow spiritually and professionally. One such student is Jerri. Through her work with women in prison and the justice system, I perceive Jerri as embodying inner work and good work—that is, work that cultivates spiritual development in oneself and others and work that enables people to use their unique talents in the service of others (Krone, 2001). I have been not only a guide for Jerri's work but the beneficiary too. Yet there is little written about mentor-mentee relationships as a place where spirituality enhances relationships in ways unaccounted for by research and practice.

Spirituality offers a range of connections—to oneself, others, organizations, a higher being—that may shift over the course of an individual's lifetime (Buzzanell, 2001; Lesser, 1999; Sass, 2000). The spiritual values of compassion, humility, and simplicity are a basis on which spiritual practices and identities form and grow. In turn, practices and identities shape the meanings and enactments of values. To discuss how individuals engage in spiritual mentor-mentee relationships, I present an overview of mentoring literature and comment on the roles of spirituality and religion in inner and good work. Mentoring should be linked to spiritual values, so that development of the whole person can be undertaken in both relational roles.

New Directions for Teaching and Learning, no. 120, Winter 2009 © Wiley Periodicals, Inc.
Published online in Wiley InterScience (www.interscience.wiley.com) • DOI: 10.1002/tl.373

Spiritual Mentoring in Practice: Teacher-Student Relations

I compare and contrast the main issues and findings in traditional and spiritual mentoring before situating spiritual mentoring in career theory, research, and practice.

Mentoring, Traditional and Spiritual. Mentoring traditionally is considered to be the one-on-one professional development of someone less experienced by a wiser, older, and more experienced person. Although individualized teaching still occurs in real-time venues, we live in an era in which mentoring is accomplished by numerous means, including being mediated by technologies through online support, e-mentoring, and related venues. Mentoring has expanded from face-to-face negotiations and learning to a more diverse range of activities, attachments, and forms (Ragins and Kram, 2007).

Although the diverse forms (formal or informal), functions (psychosocial, career, role modeling), results (positive or negative), contexts (face-to-face dyadic, cluster, online), and directions (downward, reverse, peer) of mentoring have been documented (Allen and others, 2004; Hall and Associates, 1996), the core still is expertise sharing. The motivation for such relationships is that they are stipulated by employment contracts, or that one party needs advice and another wants to build a legacy and impart knowledge. For spiritual mentoring, however, motivation transcends workplace benefits.

There has been little discussion of spiritual mentoring except for guidance in how to relate to a higher being. Especially in institutions of higher education—as in faith-based colleges—the emphasis is on alignment of university mission with everyday spiritual acts (Feldner, 2006); tensions that arise among competing religious, spiritual, and institutional values and practices (Kirby and others, 2006); and how members enact their calling to guide students in their connection with God and meaningful work (Scott, 2007). Others' guidance in spiritual quest is one notion of spiritual mentoring, but it is not the definition used in this essay.

Instead, spiritual mentoring refers to a particular way of interacting in mentor-mentee relationships. Spiritual mentoring transcends the usual career, psychosocial support, and role-modeling activities to embrace the whole person. Spiritual mentoring might mean that teachers/mentors reframe their job so as to assist in cultivating both their own spiritual development and/or that of others. For example, Palmer (2003) summarized the case of a teacher, Mr. Porter, who made a difference in a child's life through nurturing the child and the child's gifts. Porter's care of the child was not only his own good work in that he enabled the child to appreciate and develop unique talents, but he also showed the child how to mentor others. In spiritual mentoring, the true vocation is the ongoing work of developing both parties' spirituality, with the mentor guiding the process at some times and the mentee directing it at others. Spirituality offers a process for encouraging inner and good work within the interactions.

NEW DIRECTIONS FOR TEACHING AND LEARNING • DOI: 10.1002/tl

Situating Spiritual Mentoring in Career

Within most career research and practice, mentoring is known as a key learning strategy for improving competence evaluations, advancement opportunities, and secure employability (Allen, Day, and Lentz, 2005). Knowing *who* along with knowing *what* and *how* enhances career capital (Arthur, Inkson, and Pringle, 1999). Developing relationships, meta-skills, and spirituality can act as a hedge against the uncertainties of a precarious psychological contract between employer and employee or entrepreneur (Arthur, Inkson, and Pringle, 1999; Buzzanell, 2001; Hall and Associates, 1996). As such, spirituality can be considered a tool for increasing stability and coherence in uncertain times (Buzzanell, 2002).

When spirituality is seen as an inherent process within everyday life, then it encourages reevaluation of work and career. This reevaluation focuses attention on how people live and question the values that are the cornerstone for spirituality, and it locates practices that infuse the mundane with spirituality (Buzzanell, 2001; Harlos, 2000). Many of us recall reevaluating our lives at a time of tragedy, such as September 11, 2001 (Buzzanell, 2002), and now in the upsurge of global economic instability (Miller, 2009). Spirituality also enables us—as researchers, teachers, and organizational members—to transform the definition of career from sequences of work-related experiences or contracts to a more inclusive definition. Thus career becomes "an expansive discourse through which work acquires coherence and meaning in individuals' lives" (Buzzanell and Lucas, 2006, p. 172).

It is in spiritual practice that spirituality, career, and mentoring coalesce. Spiritual practice challenges people to express their individual spirituality in ordinary life as well as in determining how such actions might move them and others closer to, or further away from, higher-order, community, or self-connections. With regard to spiritual mentoring, the mentor-mentee relationship may resemble friendship models of teaching, advising, and co-learning (Buell, 2004; Rawlins, 2000) as students and mentors grow and share advice (Waldeck, Oggero, Plax, and Kearney, 1997).

Connections of Religion and Spirituality to Inner Work and Good Work

In working with students, I often ask them to write their reasons for doing a project and where they see themselves in their project. I ask how the project relates to other work so that there is coherence and meaning in students' lives and careers. These questions drove my interactions with Jerri about her thesis (Faris, 2006). Her written responses and subsequent reflections on her answers became the opening and closing prayers that bracketed her thesis and that, indeed, seem to have framed our co-mentoring relationship as well as her spiritual mentoring of others.

Spirituality and Religion. Religion provides answers in the form of doctrine, whereas spirituality focuses on "a reality beyond the material" (Daniels, Franz, and Wong, 2000, p. 543) and connotes openness to "an 'unseen order' in the world around us . . . the drive to create wholeness" (Mirvis, 1997, p. 20). For some students like Jerri, the embodiment of religion and spirituality is closely linked and integral to their scholarship. In these cases, my aim is to help them use their gifts, challenge the religion-academic links, and integrate self, religion, spiritualities, and studies.

Actualization of Spiritual Mentoring Practices and Values. How spiritual mentoring takes place is dependent on shifting role relationships, the context in which both parties are embedded, and how they understand themselves, their goals, and their spiritualities. In this section, I discuss how spiritual mentoring can take place in institutions of higher education as well as through specific practices and spiritual values.

Enactment of Spiritual Mentor-Mentee Relationships. Graduate and undergraduate communication education is an iterative process that does not end in the classroom or in formal advising or mentoring relationships. It is a process of challenging students to develop their identities as individual scholars, teachers, and engaged community participants on the basis of their strengths, spiritualities, and interests. I integrate these activities into course content and pedagogical methods as well as in routine interactions with students. Mentoring becomes synonymous with teaching insofar as teaching involves more than transmission of a field's values and assumptions. Mentoring transcends the teaching relationship whenever both parties focus on the construction of inner and good work within the nexus of self, community, (perhaps) a higher being, and spiritual practices. Spiritual mentoring takes place in overlapping processes: offering opportunities for development, engaging in spontaneous teaching and mentoring, enlarging and enriching resources, and encouraging continuous development.

First, part of one's role as instructor and mentor is to work with students to promote opportunities for their development. If students are able to choose how they integrate work meaningfully into their lives, then spiritual mentors have succeeded. My focus is on the student and his or her interests, needs, values, and phase in the life span (my academic specialty is the conduit). The opportunities that my mentees and I co-create may translate into co-authorship, feedback sessions on teaching, ongoing conversation about both parties' work-life goals, and encouragement of students' agendas. In these ways, spiritual mentoring could be characterized as more of a facilitation, sponsorship, or servant leadership (Fine and Buzzanell, 2000; Greenleaf, 1996).

Second, spiritual mentoring may be less about the doing of formal mentoring, such as forming career strategies, than about everyday moment-by-moment processes—as spontaneous teaching, advising, and connecting. As a mundane process, spiritual mentoring may occur in hallway conversation

NEW DIRECTIONS FOR TEACHING AND LEARNING • DOI: 10.1002/tl

in which faculty members ask students how their semester is going, what they are working on, how their family is, and so on.

Students have told me that these spontaneous interactions are motivating because they sometimes wonder if anyone notices or cares about them. Personalized exchanges matter greatly. Congratulating students on their accomplishments, relating positive comments someone might have said about them, offering advice on how to navigate work-life experiences, and encouraging their questioning about their lives and decisions are ordinary ways in which spiritual mentoring occurs. These conversations may remain at the level of a quick chat or become lengthy exchanges about research papers, activities, or other issues. Hopefully, they build confidence, humanize the higher education process, and encourage students to locate the work from which they can develop their whole selves.

Most important, they help students connect to self and others. I find that students relish discussing their experiences. These exchanges are not always spiritual mentoring in the fullest sense, but they offer possibilities on which students and instructors can build. The reciprocal nature of spiritual mentoring means that these exchanges benefit both parties. I have learned a great deal about dialectic tension, irony in enactment of identity (-ies), and the need for more sophisticated treatment of work-life issues over the life span through sharing my experiences raising six children and listening to my students' discussions of their families.

Third, besides creating opportunities and engaging in spontaneous connections and advising, spiritual mentoring also means enlarging and enriching the resources upon which students can draw. As teachers we have opportunities to open our field and make contacts with others for our students. These contacts occur through other scholars' writings, but also through e-mail exchanges, and classroom visits. Chadwick and Russo (2002) describe how they become virtual visiting professors (VVR) at other universities. Their VVR is not someone who does a one-time lecture but is someone fully integrated into the course and possible future exchanges.

Fourth, spiritual mentoring means that mentors have a responsibility and commitment to continue their own spiritual development and professional discovery, learning, and engagement and to foster lifelong learning in others. Maintaining patterns of continuous seeking (in self, other, and higher being connections; see Lesser, 1999) and of career development models the behavior and thinking that spiritual mentors want to inspire in their students. Through these patterns, mentors are less likely to engage in dysfunctional mentoring because they, along with their students, are in a process of co-learning and spiritual discovery. Negative mentoring ranges from discouraging development of an idea to which a student feels a strong commitment to appropriating ideas by either party without due credit (Eby, McManus, Simon, and Russell, 2000). These behaviors can diminish a reputation or confidence.

In short, spiritual mentors incorporate the activities mentioned into graduate and undergraduate classes. They seek out students for contact, encourage a collaborative and peer mentoring atmosphere, and participate in varied educational and mentoring activities.

Embodiment of Spiritual Values. The practices just described are simply activities unless they are guided by the spiritual values of compassion, humility, and simplicity (Harlos, 2000). Compassion is "a deep concern for others expressed as helpful, kind actions requiring empathy, patience, and courage" (p. 618). Humility is a resistance to arrogance, to positioning oneself as central, and to anything that does not foster a co-learning atmosphere. In simplicity, people focus on substantive issues. They question routines that take time from important activities—activities of giving to others, mentoring, teaching, reflecting, and engaging. As mentees and mentors interact, they challenge each other so that superfluous advice or data are stripped away. What remains is a focus on what matters in life and how both parties contribute to one another's wholeness (Buzzanell, 2001).

Taken together, these spiritual values translate into an environment that respects the collaborative knowledge construction. Humility means that one can relish others' successes, without becoming concerned that they might be smarter, more insightful, or better writers.

Mentor-mentee relationships develop emotional bonds, multiple identity constructions, and spiritual drive toward meaning, connection, and wholeness (Bell, Golombisky, Singh, and Hirschmann, 2000). For many women faculty, life-changing mentoring is infused with knowing that someone cares and has one's best interests at heart, feeling connected to others, having one's worth affirmed, knowing that one is not alone, and being taught how politics operate in academic experiences. These characteristics coincide with spiritual mentoring.

In conclusion, spiritual mentoring transcends conventional mentoring forms and functions through inner and good work, embodiment of spiritual values, and enactment of everyday spiritual practices. Spiritual mentoring is enacted through such behaviors as enhancing student development, engaging in spontaneous opportunities for connection, enlarging and enriching resources, and fostering continuous development. It is through attention to the here and now that spiritual mentoring builds hope for the future.

References

Allen, T., Day, R., and Lentz, E. "The Role of Interpersonal Comfort in Mentoring Relationships." *Journal of Career Development*, 2005, *31*, 155–169.
Allen, T., and others. "Career Benefits Associated with Mentoring for Protégés: A Meta-Analysis." *Journal of Applied Psychology*, 2004, *89*, 127–136.
Arthur, M. B., Inkson, K., and Pringle, J. K. *The New Careers: Individual Action and Economic Change*. London: Sage, 1999.

Bell, E., Golombisky, K., Singh, G., and Hirschmann, K. "To All the Girls I've Loved Before: Academic Love Letters on Mentoring, Power, and Desire." *Communication Theory*, 2000, *10*, 27–47.

Buell, C. "Models of Mentoring in Communication." *Communication Education*, 2004, *53*, 56–73.

Buzzanell, P. M. "Spirituality-Centered Career Theory and Practice." In A. Rodriguez (ed.), *Essays on Spirituality and Communication*. Lanham, Md.: University Press of America, 2001.

Buzzanell, P. M. *In the Silence of Our Hearts: When Spirituality and Career Discourses Collide*. Paper presented to the Central States Communication Association. Conference held in Milwaukee, Wis., April 2002.

Buzzanell, P. M., and Lucas, K. "Gendered Stories of Career: Unfolding Discourses of Time, Space, and Identity." In B. J. Dow and J. T. Wood (eds.), *The Sage Handbook on Gender and Communication*. Thousand Oaks, Calif.: Sage, 2006.

Chadwick, S., and Russo, T. "Virtual Visiting Professors: Communicative, Pedagogical, and Technological Collaboration." In P. Comeaux (ed.), *Communication and Collaboration in the Online Classroom*. Bolton, Mass.: Anker, 2002.

Daniels, D., Franz, R. S., and Wong, K. "A Classroom with a Worldview: Making Spiritual Assumptions Explicit in Management Education." *Journal of Management Education*, 2000, *24*, 540–561.

Eby, L., McManus, S. E., Simon, S. A., and Russell, J. "The Protégé's Perspective Regarding Negative Mentoring Experiences: The Development of a Taxonomy." *Journal of Vocational Behavior*, 2000, *57*, 1–21.

Faris, J. L. *Women in Jail: Putting Communication Training to Work*. Unpublished master's thesis, Purdue University, West Lafayette, Ind., 2006.

Feldner, S. B. "Living Our Mission: A Study of University Mission Building." *Communication Studies*, 2006, *57*, 67–85.

Fine, M., and Buzzanell, P. M. "Walking the High Wire: Leadership Theorizing, Daily Acts, and Tensions." In P. M. Buzzanell (ed.), *Rethinking Organizational and Managerial Communication from Feminist Perspectives*. Thousand Oaks, Calif.: Sage, 2000.

Greenleaf, R. K. *On Becoming a Servant Leader*. San Francisco: Jossey-Bass, 1996.

Hall, D. T., and Associates (eds.). *The Career Is Dead—Long Live the Career: A Relational Approach to Careers*. San Francisco: Jossey-Bass, 1996.

Harlos, K. P. "Toward a Spiritual Pedagogy: Meaning, Practice, and Applications in Management Education." *Journal of Management Education*, 2000, *24*, 612–627.

Kirby, E. L., and others. "The Jesuit Difference (?): Tensions of Negotiating Spiritual Values and Secular Practices." *Communication Studies*, 2006, *57*, 87–105.

Krone, K. "Reframing Organizational Communication Theory and Research Through Spirituality." In A. Rodriguez (ed.), *Essays on Spirituality and Communication*. Lanham, Md.: University Press of America, 2001.

Lesser, E. *The New American Spirituality: A Seeker's Guide*. New York: Random House, 1999.

Miller, L. "Divine Refuge in the Storm." *Newsweek*, Feb. 16, 2009, p. 15.

Mirvis, P. H. "'Soul Work' in Organizations." *Organization Science*, 1997, *8*, 193–206.

Palmer, P. J. "Teaching with Heart and Soul: Reflections on Spirituality in Teacher Education." *Journal of Teacher Education*, 2003, *54*, 376–385.

Ragins, B. R., and Kram, K. E. *The Handbook of Mentoring at Work: Theory, Research, and Practice*. Thousand Oaks, Calif.: Sage, 2007.

Rawlins, W. "Teaching as a Mode of Friendship." *Communication Theory*, 2000, *10*, 5–26.

Sass, J. S. "Characterizing Organizational Spirituality: An Organizational Communication Culture Approach." *Communication Studies*, 2000, *51*, 195–217.

Scott, J. A. "Our Callings, Our Selves: Repositioning Religious and Entrepreneurial Discourses in Career Theory and Practice." *Communication Studies*, 2007, *58*, 261–279.

Waldeck, J., Oggero, V. O., Plax, T. G., and Kearney, P. "Graduate Student/Faculty Mentoring Relationships: Who Gets Mentored, How It Happens, and to What End." *Communication Quarterly*, 1997, *45*, 93–109.

PATRICE M. BUZZANELL *is professor and the W. Charles and Ann Redding Faculty Fellow in the Department of Communication at Purdue University. Her research interests center on the construction of gendered workplace identities, interactions, and structures, particularly as they relate to career and leadership processes. She has edited or co-edited three books and published in numerous journals.*

NEW DIRECTIONS FOR TEACHING AND LEARNING • DOI: 10.1002/tl

4

In this chapter, Hamlet discusses the nature of her spirituality and how it informs and affects her teaching philosophy and pedagogical practices in the multicultural classroom, especially in teaching an intercultural communication course.

Engaging Spirituality and an Authentic Self in the Intercultural Communication Class

Janice D. Hamlet

Intercultural communication focuses on understanding the relationship between culture and communication. The goal of such understanding is to assist students in developing awareness, competency, and sensitivity in communicating with persons who have cultural backgrounds (and perspectives) different from their own, or what Young Yun Kim (2001) refers to as *intercultural personhood*: a way of life that is called for by the increasingly intercultural realities of our world. The intercultural person is a type whose cognitive, affective, and behavioral characteristics are not limited but open to growth beyond the psychological parameters of his or her culture. It is a journey that both students and the professor take. There is no better way to describe and assess this experience than through the autoethnographic narrative. The emergence of autoethnography as a method of inquiry moves researchers' use of self-observation as part of the situation studied to self-introspection or self-ethnography as a legitimate focus of study in and of itself (Ellis, 1991).

In this autoethnography, I discuss how my spirituality and cultural identity informs and affects my teaching philosophy and pedagogical practices, especially in the teaching of intercultural communication.

NEW DIRECTIONS FOR TEACHING AND LEARNING, no. 120, Winter 2009 © Wiley Periodicals, Inc.
Published online in Wiley InterScience (www.interscience.wiley.com) • DOI: 10.1002/tl.374

Intercultural Communication Class: Fall 2008

One autumn evening during the early part of fall semester 2008, following my intercultural communication class, I experienced this incredible feeling of satisfaction, calmness, and peace as I reflected on that evening's session on my way home. The class session had focused on cultural awareness, sensitivity, and community. The thirty-six students sat in a big circle and were instructed to respond to statements that I read aloud, by standing if the statements referred to them. They were not allowed to speak. They were to remain standing (while looking around to see who else was standing or not standing) until I asked them to be seated. I also informed the class that they had the right not to respond to any statements, but their honesty would be appreciated and would lead them to greater self-awareness and sensitivity toward others, and in helping all of us come together as a class. The activity afforded an opportunity for these thirty-six strangers—representing both genders, various ages, nontraditional students, different ethnic backgrounds, nationalities, sexual orientations, religious beliefs and practices—to discover one another's commonalities, differences, and shortcomings. To my surprise, everyone participated, even as the experience became more challenging with each new statement.

Following the "big circle activity," the students broke up into smaller groups where they had an opportunity to explain their backgrounds and experiences that may have affected why they stood or didn't stand when certain statements were read during the activity. In the process of discovery, the community building that took root in the circle started to grow. The students bonded. Afterward, there was discussion, laughter, tears, handshakes, and a lot of hugs. It was a revealing, intense activity that resulted in catharsis and harmony. I shared in their excitement, but for my own reasons. I had done this activity before in my intercultural communication classes, but never with total participation nor this type of bonding. They got what I was trying to achieve, and it was gratifying, harmonious, and spiritual.

The Nature of My Spirituality. *Spirituality*, as I embrace it, refers to my acceptance and acknowledgment of God as the source of my existence and strength. This belief in a connection to a higher power enables me to overcome the limitations of my physical mind and body and experience worthiness, security, empowerment, and peace. How I connect with my spirit is intimately connected to my cultural identity. I am African American. I believe, as noted by Carlyle Stewart (1999), that spirituality is also a process by which people interpret, disclose, formulate, adapt, and innovate reality and their understandings of God within a specific context or culture. It signifies a mode of existence that creates its own praxis and culture and compels identification and resolution of human problems through divine intervention. Stewart writes about spirituality from an African American cultural perspective, reinforcing that one of the most significant elements shaping the identity of African Americans is the will to survive, a

NEW DIRECTIONS FOR TEACHING AND LEARNING • DOI: 10.1002/tl

desire to confront and surmount threats to their being and existence while concurrently creating idioms of life and culture that give them adaptive mechanisms to reinforce their sanity, affirm their wholeness, and establish their spiritual and ontological location in American society (Stewart, 1997). This idea about the connection between culture and spirituality is a natural manifestation of African American people's history and legacy of survival. As a result, it is something far more powerful than religious or institutional affiliation.

My spiritual practices include the daily ritual of prayer. I've learned that this earthly journey is a lot easier to navigate if you pray along the way. The campus shootings at my university on February 14, 2008, reinforced for me that each day is a blessing and should never be taken for granted. Other activities reinforce or complement my connection to the spirit, such as my daily drive to campus being enhanced with musical renditions from my favorite gospel artists blasting from the car's CD player. The music puts me in a good mood for the day (or at least the morning). My morning ritual is complete after I arrive in my office, water the plants, make coffee (this is not a spiritual practice but a necessary one), and then read a scripture card from the elegant porcelain box that sits on my desk. I'm now ready to begin my work day with the belief that I will have divine guidance and intervention with whatever I have to confront that day, especially in the classroom.

Engaging Spirituality in the Classroom. I enter my classroom with the challenge of building communality among my students in order to create a climate of openness, respect, and comfortableness as well as intellectual rigor. I encourage open communication by encouraging students to share their experiences and how they interpret them, and to understand the roots of their interpretation. I value student expression and the diversity of persons, experiences, and perspectives. I also seek to establish an environment whereby my students and I can learn from each other. I have learned from social critic Bell Hooks (1994) that seeing the classroom as a communal place enhances the likelihood of collective effort in creating and sustaining a learning community. I have also learned that communality is enhanced when I bring my authentic self to the classroom and use all aspects of my identity to inform and engage my students in my efforts to facilitate learning. *Authenticity* in the context of teaching refers to a way of speaking and behaving that is consistent with one's personal and cultural ethos, identity, and beliefs. It is the ability to consistently use one's own voice, one's language, to communicate with power, clarity, courage, and sincerity in the service of helping others reach their highest potential, not only as professionals but as human beings. In essence, "when you know who you are from the inside out; when you do what you sense is right for you regardless of what others are saying or doing; when your first point of reference is your own thought; and, when your thoughts lead you to actions which serve others as well as make you feel good, you have encountered spirituality" (Vanzant, 1992, p. 19).

Intercultural Communication Class: Fall 2007

As a course activity, this particular semester students were required to introduce themselves to the class by discussing their cultural background and
bringing an artifact to class that represented something about them. I was
amazed at what students brought in: pieces of fine china that belonged to
great-great-grandparents who had brought them with them when they came
to this country; clocks, jewelry, quilts, clothing, photos. Like many activities
I assigned, I also participated. At the end of the last round of presentations, I
walked to the front of the room carrying two items shielded in bubble wrap.
Before I unwrapped the first item, I shared with the class a little about my cultural background and the values that had been instilled in me from my parents. I also talked about my belief in angels and why I believed in their
existence. After this discussion, I exposed the first item, a small black angel
that stood about four inches tall. I explained that I had owned the angel since
the age of five, a peace offering from my mother following a shopping trip she
took with my Dad. As the family story goes, I had received a spanking from
my Dad after throwing a temper tantrum when I discovered that I would not
be accompanying my parents on this particular shopping trip, as was usually
the case. I had to stay home with my older siblings. On their return, the little black angel was given to me with a card attached on which my mother had
written: *Even when you act ugly, you are still my little black angel. Love Mother.*
It was the first time I had seen a black angel and I adored it. I explained that
as a result of my numerous career moves, the card got lost, but the angel is
one of my most treasured possessions. Some thirty years later, my mother,
now retired and taking arts and craft classes at the neighborhood community
center, made me a larger version of the little black angel. My dad informed
me that my mother was so moved that I had kept the little store-bought angel
all these years, she wanted to make me one. With that statement, I unwrapped the larger black angel for the class to see. I explained how much the
angels meant to me and how these two angels and a health crisis in 1994 had
motivated me to start collecting black angels. I ended the presentation by
informing the class that by the year 2000, I had collected more than two hundred black angels, in addition to several other angels that represented other
ethnic groups. The presentation led to students sharing stories about their or
their parents' collection activities. I enjoyed it. My participation in the assignment allowed the class to know who I was from a cultural perspective, just
as I had learned something about them. It was an opportunity to contribute
to the interplay between culture and communication in the classroom.
Engaging spirituality in the classroom has become the path to my own eman-
cipation in which my intellectual life, cultural identity, and spirit merge.

Leading students to intercultural personhood is a noble cause. But like
all noble causes, it requires risk taking, which oftentimes results in a price
one has to pay. The multicultural classroom is phenomenal in terms of what
students offer to course content. But when the course curriculum is inter-

NEW DIRECTIONS FOR TEACHING AND LEARNING • DOI: 10.1002/tl

cultural communication, with a focus on challenging students' deep-seated beliefs—many of which are prejudices, stereotypes, and biases toward other groups of people that have been taught in the home or a community environment—the multicultural classroom becomes not only challenging but also problematic. It is especially problematic when the teacher is a person of color in a predominantly white classroom. Sometimes white students feel a bit uncomfortable with my pedagogical approach because I celebrate my cultural identity, and my approach forces them out of their comfort zone. Students of color, especially African American students, often appreciate this approach but get agitated when white students make comments that they find offensive and expect me to "attack" them on their behalf. They are disappointed when I don't.

Intercultural Communication Class: Fall 2002

It was the first day of the semester for my intercultural communication course. After introducing myself and explaining a little about the course, I instructed students to arrange their seats in a circle. They were simply assigned to introduce themselves and inform everyone why they were taking the course. Things were going smoothly and routinely as I continued to hear students announce that they were taking the course as an elective to complete their major, or because the day and time of the course fit with their existing schedule. A few said they heard it was a good course and another group announced that they had me before and like the way I taught. But I wasn't hearing the statement that I always hope to hear on the first day: "I want to be more tolerant of people different from me," or "I want to be better prepared to interact with different people in the workplace," or anything that had to do with being a better person.

Finally, we reached a white female who, after giving her name, made this startling statement: "I'm really happy to be in this class with so many minorities. I always tell my friends that my mother must have been a black woman in another life because she sure can fry chicken. I love my mother's fried chicken!" I desperately tried to keep my composure as I exclaimed silently, *O my God! It's just the first day!* By the very nature of the course and my pedagogical approach, I usually anticipate that students will make statements that may offend, or simply annoy, other students. But this usually comes farther along in the semester. As I looked at the student, I couldn't help but also see the two African American females who sat next to her. Their chins had lowered and they had cast a deadly stare at the student, then at me. But they remained silent. However, the African American male student seated next to me couldn't hold his tongue. He asked, "What the hell do Black women have to do with frying chicken? I've never seen a black woman on a box of chicken, but I have seen Colonel Sanders on the Kentucky Fried Chicken box and I have seen a picture of Frank Portillo on the Brown's chicken box [a Chicago chain of restaurants]. Dr. Hamlet, do you know what she's talking about?" I knew that by directing the question to me he was expecting me to straighten this student out. The other African American students looked at me as if they were all saying, "Yeah, Dr. Hamlet, tell her off." Truth be told, I was just as insulted by the statement as they were, but I knew that I couldn't go off on the student as the African American students hoped. I had to be the facilitator, the teacher. But I needed divine intervention. I quietly asked spirit to come in and take over.

While still trying to maintain my composure, I asked the white female if she would explain what she meant by her statement. The student, who at this point was fighting back tears, said the cooks at her high school cafeteria had all been mostly African American women and they always provided delicious meals, fried chicken being one of them, which was usually served at banquets and other school activities. Her mother, unlike a lot of her friends' mothers, could also make very good fried chicken. Therefore she had something in common with these African American women. She said she thought she was giving a compliment and apologized if she had offended. This was followed by a statement from one of the African American females who had given her (and me) a deadly stare: "Well, you should be more careful when you make a statement like that because not all black women can cook." Another African American student was about to comment when I interrupted. "OK, OK," I said. I thanked the white student for her clarification of the statement, and I thanked the African American male and female students for their comments and then said, "Let's continue with the introductions, and then I want to talk about what just happened and what will likely happen the rest of the semester."

Following the introductions, I proceeded to talk about the course and how our attention would be focused on understanding the nature of prejudice, recognizing stereotypes and the damage they can do to others, the power of language, and celebrating cultural differences as well as those variables that we all have in common. I also indicated that if this course was to be successful, we must allow our students to express themselves: "You will say things that may offend other students, and you will be allowed to voice how you feel about what someone else said, including me. However, I expect you to communicate in a way that does not destroy your classmates, that does not rob them of their dignity, their spirit."

I ended the class session with a quote from Dr. Martin Luther King, Jr., that also appeared at the top of the course syllabus. I thought the class had ended on a good note, only to discover, through e-mail messages, that the two African American female students who had given me the deadly stares felt I should have told the white female off for her statement, particularly since I too am an African American woman. It would take the rest of the semester for them to understand the choice I made that day. From being introduced to important terms and theoretical concepts illustrated through role plays, simulations, group activities and presentations, tests, papers, film presentations, guest speakers, and so on, they finally got the message.

NEW DIRECTIONS FOR TEACHING AND LEARNING • DOI: 10.1002/tl

Intercultural Communication Graduate Seminar: Spring 2005

In this graduate seminar on intercultural communication, the students, like graduate students in previous semesters, admitted they had never taken a course focusing on intercultural communication. So I felt that it was important to introduce them to general background information before getting into a discussion about theories and conducting research in this area. It made sense to me, and previous seminars had gone well because of it. But it didn't make sense to this particular group of students. Because they were "graduate students" they felt that I should only be teaching them about theories and presenting "scholarly" materials to them. Additionally, the idea of thinking about the relevance of a theory and its application to their personal and future professional lives seemed elementary and irrelevant to them. As a result, although I was complimented on being a "nice person," the majority of the students in the seminar expressed disappointment in my teaching method and the seminar. I failed in my attempt with this class to help them understand that studying theory without understanding its usefulness in their social interactions is worthless. But I also forgot that what may work with one group may not necessarily work with another. The experience reminded me that I must be willing to revise and come up with fresh, innovative ways to teach the same subject matter. A spirituality developed in the context of a teaching life would have to strive to maintain an ongoing openness toward new and diverse ways of letting people learn, but especially toward letting oneself learn how to let others learn, in such a way that one would progressively become transparent to what one intends to let others learn, so that in "seeing" the teacher they would learn the taught [Gotz, 1997, p. 5].

Reflections

From these and other experiences, I have learned that it takes effort, time, motivation, energy, creativity, patience, practice, and a lot of prayer to build communality among diverse students. But it is an opportunity to allow spirit to come in and empower you and, as a result, touch lives, including your own.

I have been informed and encouraged by the work of Kathleen Talvacchia (2003), who advocates for a spirituality of multiculturally sensitive teaching. Multiculturally sensitive teaching, notes Talvacchia, demands the formation of the teacher as a professional who forms herself spiritually as a person who is able to relate openly to her students in their totality as human beings. Ignoring the role of spirituality in one's personal development and professional behavior is to overlook a potentially powerful avenue through which people construct meaning and knowledge (Tisdell,

2001). The spiritual component of human beings that gives rise to questions about why we do what we do pushes us to seek fundamentally better ways of doing it and propels us to make a difference in the world (Zohar and Marshall, 2004).

Intercultural Communication Class: Fall 2008. After a wonderful, often intense semester of learning and sharing about cultural concepts, theories, and experiences, especially the campaign and election of the nation's first African American president, the course, like most courses, culminated with a final exam. However, before the final exam was distributed, I played then-President-elect Barack Obama's election night victory speech, one that acknowledged the diversity of the people who got him elected. Although I knew the students had already heard it, I acknowledged that it was a fitting end to this course focusing on diversity. Said Obama:

> If there is anyone out there who still doubts that America is a place where all things are possible; who still wonders if the dream of our founders is alive in our time; who still questions the power of our democracy, tonight is your answer.
>
> It's the answer told by lines that stretched around schools and churches in numbers this nation has never seen; by people who waited three hours and four hours, many for the very first time in their lives, because they believed that this time must be different; that their voice could be that difference.
>
> It's the answer spoken by young and old, rich and poor, Democrat and Republican, black, white, Hispanic, Asian, Native American, gay, straight, disabled and not disabled—Americans who sent a message to the world that we have ever never been a collection of Red States and Blue States; we are, and always will be, the United States of America.
>
> It's the answer that led those who have been told for so long by so many to be cynical, and fearful, and doubtful of what we can achieve to put their hands on the arc of history and bend it once more toward the hope of a better day. It's been a long time coming, but tonight, because of what we did on this day, in this election, at this defining moment, change has come to America. [Obama, 2008, n.p.]

Following the speech, there was applause. I added that Obama's landslide victory was a wonderful indication of what America is capable of achieving despite the naysayers and hatemongers. I thanked the class for taking this intercultural communication journey with me. I announced that I wanted to leave them with one final thought, a quote from Gandhi: "You be the change you wish to see in the world."

References

Ellis, C. "Sociological Introspection and Emotional Experience." *Symbolic Interaction*, 1991, *14*, 23–50.

Gotz, I. L. On Spirituality and Teaching, Philosophy of Education, 1997. Retrieved from http: www.ed.uiuc.edu/EPS/PES-Yearbook/97-docs/gotz.html

Hooks, B. *Teaching to Transgress: Education as the Practice of Freedom.* New York: Routledge, 1994.
Kim, Y. Y. "Toward Intercultural Personhood: An Integration of Eastern and Western Perspectives." In L. A. Samovar, R. E. Porter, and E. R. McDaniel (eds.), *Intercultural Communication: A Reader.* Boston: Wadsworth, 2001.
Obama, B. Acceptance Speech, Grant Park, Chicago, Illinois, Nov. 4, 2008.
Stewart, C. F. *Soul Survivors: An African American Spirituality.* Louisville, Ky.: Westminster John Knox Press, 1997.
Stewart, C. F. *Black Spirituality and Black Consciousness.* Trenton, N.J.: Africa World Press, 1999.
Talvacchia, K. T. *Critical Minds and Discerning Hearts: A Spirituality of Multicultural Teaching.* St. Louis, Mo.: Chalice Press, 2003.
Tisdell, E. J. "Spirituality in Adult and Higher Education." In ERIC Clearinghouse on Adult Career and Vocational Education. Columbus, Ohio, 2001.
Vanzant, I. L. *Tapping the Power Within: A Path to Self-Empowerment for Black Women.* New York: Harlem River Press, 1992.
Zohar, D., and Marshall, I. *Spiritual Capital: Wealth We Can Live By.* San Francisco: Berrett-Koehler, 2004.

JANICE D. HAMLET is an associate professor of communication at Northern Illinois University in DeKalb, Illinois. Hamlet's research interests focus on African American culture and rhetoric, womanist epistemology and theology, rhetorical theory and criticism, and culture and pedagogy. She teaches intercultural communication, rhetorical theory, and criticism and has edited two books and published in numerous journals and edited volumes.

SECTION TWO

Spirituality as Self-Discovery and Insight

5

Can one appropriately teach with the spirit in a secular classroom? This chapter addresses the question by exploring how the concepts of serendipity and stewardship encourage a form of spirituality that is inclusive and appropriate for the university setting.

Serendipity and Stewardship: Teaching with the Spirit in a Secular Classroom

By Bradford "J" Hall

I have always considered spirituality an important part of life but have been somewhat cautious in terms of how it is played out in the classroom. Spirituality can be linked to specific religious traditions in ways that create exclusion, rather than the inclusion I prefer and believe should exist in state-sponsored universities. However, after reading a book edited by Denton and Ashton (2004), I was struck by the classroom really being a "site" where one's personal and professional life connect. This connection may not always be explicitly evident, and I may not have framed it in this way before, but I believe I inherently involve my sense of spirituality in any classroom. I suspect we all do more than we realize.

In considering spirituality in the classroom, I am going to stray far afield from my usual writing and research and explicitly consider how the spirit communicates within an educational context. My understanding of the spirit suggests that teaching is one of its basic functions (John 14:26, Holy Bible: Authorized King James Version, the scriptural source cited throughout this chapter); however, working with the spirit in the classroom can be a challenge. The first thing that came to mind when I considered this issue is the scripture in the Bible where Jesus is explaining spiritual rebirth to Nicodemus: "The wind bloweth where it listeth, and thou hearest the sound thereof, but canst not tell whence it cometh, and whither it goeth; so is everyone that is born of the Spirit" (John 3: 8). Pinning down how the spirit communicates is a process fraught with ambiguity and uncertainty. However, my experience suggests that two concepts, serendipity and stewardship, can help garner and

NEW DIRECTIONS FOR TEACHING AND LEARNING, no. 120, Winter 2009 © Wiley Periodicals, Inc.
Published online in Wiley InterScience (www.interscience.wiley.com) • DOI: 10.1002/tl.375

direct the power of the spirit when explicitly made a part of the classroom, just as the windmill does with the wind.

Serendipity

Serendipity refers to unexpected but joyful finds or discoveries. A small example can be seen in a recent visit with a graduate student. She came to my office to ask about administrative information related to organizing a new course proposal. I was able to direct her to the information she needed, and then I asked about the nature of her course. She explained that it was focused on communication differences between Germans and Americans. That reminded me of a book I have on the topic, and I lent it to her. She was very pleased and has found it to be very useful. She came in looking for one thing but ended up with an unexpected find that proved even more valuable than her original request. Serendipity happens at unexpected times, and though at one level it may seem a contradictory notion, I try to build it into the courses I teach.

I encourage serendipity by creating opportunities for unexpected learning to occur in my classroom. I am reminded of one such instance in which I was teaching an intercultural communication class. It was near the end of the summer session, and we had just covered some issues related to ethics. I told a fable in which a young Japanese boy is able to befriend a dragon. The story itself has many interpretations and therefore is an example of an activity ripe with potential serendipities. One of the students then asked what my perspective in this area was based on and why I took the position that I did. I don't remember the specifics, but I gave a brief (and perhaps pat-sounding) reply that did not satisfy the student, and he continued to probe. It struck me as he asked his questions that really my own concerns in this area were grounded in my personal belief, in a very real sense, that we are all children of God. So I briefly explained my belief. This explanation was surprising to the class. For some it was very positive and for others perplexing. In any case, the genuineness of the explanation and discussion around it satisfied the student and provided food for thought for all involved.

Planning for Serendipity. I frequently incorporate activities into the classroom that are not exactly what they seem. For example, Barnga is a card game in which groups of players get differing sets of rules without knowing it. After an initial learning stage, the card game is played in silence, so participants often do not realize the source of their difficulties for some time, if at all. Students learn about hidden assumptions and the danger of hasty judgment in a way that is emotionally surprising. In another class, we do an activity that is explicitly concerned with education and personality-based learning styles. However, the types and categories are completely fictitious. Students take a test to "determine" their learning personality, but they are assigned to groups purely randomly. The structure of the activity quickly has students shaping their self-description and attitude in a way that matches

NEW DIRECTIONS FOR TEACHING AND LEARNING • DOI: 10.1002/tl

their randomly assigned personality. Afterward, students frequently comment that they appreciate (or feel) the power of labels as they never had before. I believe that part of this is, because they were not expecting to learn about the power of labels, it came to them as a surprise.

Another type of activity that can generate serendipity is when students themselves furnish the data on which findings are built. For example, I require my students to connect to class concepts by frequently writing narratives that illustrate or challenge the concepts we are exploring. These papers have prompted and documented a variety of serendipities over the years. In addition, I gather information from students that have multiple uses (some more obvious than others). In another example, in a class I teach on language, thought, and behavior I have the students videotaped doing a few role plays. These role plays are used at different points throughout the semester as we look at issues related to power, social accounting practices, gender, and persuasion. That this material comes from them, rather than from some distant group, always makes these later discussions much more powerful. I have also found that by doing these role plays before we explicitly discuss some of the later issues on gender, power, or prejudice, the findings are much more telling than those that occur when the students are thinking about the concepts and monitoring their speech.

All of the activities discussed here allow the spirit to work in the classroom because they permit the students to learn concepts in a way that connects to where they are in life (and not all students are in the same place), rather than simply memorizing what is important from the perspective of the professor. Thus, planning for serendipity refers to a focus on process that allows the spirit to go "whither it goeth."

Serendipity: Emotion, Cognition, Spirit, and the Creation of Joy. One common theme running through all these activities and many others is that an unexpected emotional understanding of the issue has been added to the students' cognitive understanding. The idea that they knew this material but didn't really know it is common in the feedback I get from students in these courses. Serendipity, though, should not be thought of as simply a technique or trick to surprise; instead it is an attitude of openness that resists static conceptions of knowledge and pedagogy. This form of learning is not without risks. Expression of emotion creates an uncertain environment and requires thorough debriefing if it is to build on the potential joys and benefits of the unexpected feelings and insights. The first time I did the activity where the students represent economic, social, and cultural groups, I felt pressed for time and short-changed the debriefing session. Many in the class held onto emotions facilitated by the activity for most of the semester and continued using some of the labels made up purely for the activity. I had to revisit it more than once before the class could discover the joy of learning associated with the experience. I have explicitly used that difficult class experience to help me debrief this experience for many years now, and it has proven invaluable. The opportunity for students to hear about my own mistakes and those of past students in a general sense allows them to frame the emotional experience productively, avoiding dysfunctional frames.

Students from many years ago tell me that they still remember experiences they had in my class. I take this memory to be an expression and outcome of the spirit that was in the class and interwoven into the activity remembered. Schram noted that the Torah teaches that the heart is "the seat of all memory and recollection" (2004, p. 77). If the learning that goes on in a classroom is going to have the power to be remembered, it must touch the heart in some way. The emotional connection from such experiences activates the spirit in the classroom and goes beyond the typical temporary "memorize and forget" experience that so often happens in classrooms that never leave the necessary but insufficient cognitive level. However, emotion itself is also insufficient for serendipity that connects with the spirit. The spirit connects us to a larger purpose and sensibility. Serendipities that connect with the spirit mediate emotional and cognitive knowledge in ways that generate wisdom and joy. This is why the lasting value of an emotional experience is shaped by the cognitive soil in which it is planted and nurtured.

Teaching for serendipity is not just about unexpected learning; it is about joy. Teachers are in a better position to experience and encourage serendipity when they enjoy the classroom. I am not talking about momentary pleasures. The joy that is found in this learning environment is not dependent on the specific emotions of the moment, but on the memories and knowledge that allow us all to meet the future just a little more wisely. The joy that remains from this approach to teaching lasts for many years, despite the struggles and disappointments teachers face. This is not teaching directed toward having fun or toward covering a set amount of material and wrapping up the end of the semester. It is directed toward creating lifelong resources for the students.

Knowing that I expect serendipitous experiences to be part of the learning experience in my classes creates a deep sense of responsibility in my heart and underscores the importance of the second concept I wish to discuss in this essay, stewardship. Eyre (1990) contrasts three attitudes as they relate to material goods: rentership, ownership, and stewardship. I find this distinction to also be particularly useful in considering my role in the classroom. I understand that different connotations could be brought to mind with these three terms, but I will highlight the ones I think are important in terms of teaching with the spirit.

Three Perspectives Toward the Classroom

Rentership.   Renting involves payment for the use of something that is not yours and has only temporary benefit to you. It is often done with the aspiration of moving on to something better, something that is viewed as more your own. A rentership perspective sees teaching in the classroom as something that must be done now in order to do better things, your own things, later. The classroom is just a place to stay in between opportunities to do your own work, your real work, your research (see Schwehn, 1993). Someone who takes a *just renting* approach to teaching is unlikely to get too invested in what she is doing and in the lives of the students who share the classroom with her. Thus planning tends to be done with as little effort as possible. The thought process, though typically not overt, goes something like, "That payment is made; now I can get to my real work, the work of research and publication." The rentership approach to teaching involves very little concern, if any, about what the students gain from the class.

The students in this perspective become a kind of means to an end. The rentership-based teacher uses the students to justify his or her status as a professor and considers them a necessary evil along the pathway to tenure and other promotions. Students, however, can be useful for the work of research. The renter-oriented teacher can use them to help get research data and thus accomplish other long-term goals. From this perspective, activities designed to generate serendipity are beneficial only because they allow the teacher to fill up time in the classroom. Besides, if the students have "fun" or get good grades, perhaps they will like the rentership professor better and give higher teaching evaluations, making promotions easier.

My experience with the rentership perspective has not been toward a whole course but has occurred at times with an individual class session, when I have had my mind on other things I perceived as more important. The cares of other responsibilities can at times encourage a temporary rentership perspective, as I run through the familiar motions that pass as teaching a class. In fact, I once had a student with whom I had a comfortable relationship comment that a particular class was quite interesting, but that I had seemed a bit bored, as if I had seen it all before and was just running through the motions. The comment served as a good wake-up call, because I realized that I had let myself be distracted with the cares of being a department chair and slipped into a mind-set in which I was just putting in my time. I made a very conscious effort to return to the classroom in spirit while still not forgoing my administrative responsibilities.

Ownership. There are many kinds of owners, but the basic driving forces behind this mind-set are pride and control—control in the sense that this is *your* class and *you're* the expert. This perspective finds the teacher viewing the course during the semester as a personal possession, with the teacher strictly controlling what is learned and what counts as learning. After all, the owner is the expert and really doesn't need to learn any more. In fact, ownership allows you to evaluate how good a course is simply by looking at papers that document the surface classroom experience (such as the syllabus, latest technology used, and so forth) and "outcomes," such as how low the grades are.

The students in the class are part of what is owned. These students must learn the material the ownership professor has in mind, or there is something wrong with the students. Students need to pay appropriate dues for the privilege of being in this teacher's classroom. After all, a good owner gets as much out of what he owns as he can. A good ownership teacher is always concerned about grades and making sure the grading is as rigorous as possible. It can be a real sense of pride for the owner-minded teacher to have the lowest grades around. Grades fit well with an ownership perspective because they are much more tangible and can be kept track of better than the amount of growth, knowledge, or wisdom the student develops during the class.

Because students are considered possessions, an ownership approach might cherish deeply those students who reflect well on the owner, while discarding and disparaging the rest. Although distinct in many ways from renters, owners are also interested in what students can do for the owner; therefore they may spend considerable time on aiding the right ones and even battling other teachers for the right to teach or control them.

One thing that comes with the ownership attitude is fear. Fear in the classroom, as in social interaction in general, can create a defensive attitude that resists learning (see discussions of fear in Hall, 2005; and Palmer, 2000). The fearful person is the owner, the expert, who dearly wants to make sure that others remember and respect this status. I experienced this ownership attitude and the subtle fear that accompanies it in my very first college class as a teaching assistant. With less than a week to go before the semester started, I was assigned to teach a course I had never taken and in which I had no direct interest. I was very concerned with controlling everything in the class and making sure it was not discovered that I was not the expert my official role suggested. Ideas that challenged what I had recently read from the book would not be tolerated. Fortunately, the two more experienced teaching assistants with whom I shared an office both loved teaching and loved talking about it. Their conversations, along with a more appropriate class assignment, helped me remember the love of teaching that had motivated my entry into graduate school.

Stewardship. Initially, stewardship in the classroom may be seen as the charge to convey information or knowledge about specific subjects to the students. In doing so, there is a sense that the teacher is accountable to the university that hired him or her and to the discipline in general. Certainly this accountability is there, but for me stewardship is a much deeper responsibility. Stewardship involves a trust for which a person is accountable. The spirit is best able to work in an environment of trust. Students should leave the course with memories that can be drawn on during difficult times to face life's challenges. Of course, someone could be a steward without having a stewardship perspective. To have a stewardship attitude requires a genuine involvement with and concern for that which is entrusted to your care. There is none of the lack of concern associated with the renter mind-set; nor is there the same kind of pride associated with ownership because there is a recognition that the students and the classroom are not really "yours." They are entrusted to us.

NEW DIRECTIONS FOR TEACHING AND LEARNING • DOI: 10.1002/tl

One natural question is, "For whom is the trust held?" I believe there are three deeper answers beyond the university and discipline idea noted earlier. A person does not need to accept all three; I believe acceptance of any one of them is sufficient validation of the importance of stewardship and teaching with the spirit. One answer is found in my earlier discussion of the idea that we are all children of God. There is a divine entity to which we all are accountable in terms of our relationships with others, including our students. A second answer is that of society. Our role and influence as teachers in the classroom have an impact, for good or bad, in people's lives and involve a trust that cumulatively affects the ongoing society in which we live and teach. The third answer is the students themselves. This does not mean the current students as they exist in our classroom, but the students as they will be in future years. As teachers, we are entrusted with helping to develop the knowledge, wisdom, and understanding students will carry with them in the years ahead. I am accountable to my students to do my best to prepare them in part for what lies ahead. Of course, teachers are not solitary stewards. A given student is touched by many stewards, including herself or himself.

Trinity of Stewardship

The spirit of stewardship is developed through the practice of faith, hope, and charity. I will briefly discuss these three concepts and give a short example of each.

Faith. A teacher must have faith that learning can happen in the classroom, justifying the time and care spent in preparing a variety of ways to make a difference in the students' lives. Faith is exercised through learning activities that require students to participate in the successful growth of their own knowledge and wisdom. Gibran (1981) noted that a teacher in tune with the spirit of learning "gives not of his wisdom but rather of his faith and his lovingness. If he is indeed wise he does not bid you enter the house of his wisdom, but rather leads you to the threshold of your own mind" (p. 56). The spirit of faith is also brought to the classroom as students realize that the teacher expects them to learn, expects them to stretch themselves and excel. I often write notes on my students' quizzes or papers that let them know I know they can do better or I am impressed with a particular effort. A student struggling to finish his degree told of how one of these notes helped him believe he could succeed and continue to try. I was rewarded by seeing a consistent and marked improvement in his work.

Hope. Hope is directed toward the future fruits of the faithful gardening of the moment. Hope encourages a patience and optimism that can carry a teacher through the inevitable days when no signs of progress or learning can be seen. Hope is perhaps the hardest of the three to incorporate into specific practices. A teacher can hope that the serendipities occurring in the current classroom will be harvested later, and hope is renewed when students come back with tales of that harvest.

Charity. Paul maintains that among faith, hope, and charity, charity is the greatest (see I Corinthians 12:13). Charity is the manifestation of love in the sense discussed by M. Scott Peck (1978) when he defined love as an extending of oneself for the growth of the other. Teaching by the spirit requires a person to extend oneself and be inconvenienced, not for personal credit or reward but for the benefit of others. I am reminded of the parable of the talents given by Jesus (see Matthew 25:14–30). The good stewards were those who facilitated growth with what they had been entrusted. Stewardship involves developing that love for all of the students. I have made it my practice for many years to try to learn the first names of all my students as quickly as possible. I then spend some time at a few points in the semester thinking of each student individually and trying to think of what I can do to help this person grow as an individual within the context of this class.

Charity then, as highlighted here, is not about a patronizing gift (grade or otherwise) from the privileged (teacher) to the unprivileged (student). It is about extending oneself so as to nurture positive growth in those around one. It also displays a recognition that, regardless of title, we are all in the position of student and teacher in every relationship throughout our lives. Indeed, charity or love in terms of extending ourselves for others' growth naturally fits the teacher-student relationship.

Final Thought

Serendipity and stewardship work hand in hand. Stewardship resists the temptation of turning serendipity into tricky techniques. Serendipity helps to avoid a stewardship that slips into misguided dogma, and it allows the students themselves to become stewards in their own learning. I do not believe that serendipity and stewardship are panaceas for classroom effectiveness, or that I have mastered them. However, as I have tried to put stewardship and serendipity into practice, I have learned from unexpected sources and felt a greater connection to my students and the world around me. My hope is that the ideas expressed in this chapter will prompt your own reflection into the teaching process and what role the spirit has in that process.

References

Denton, D., and Ashton, W. *Spirituality, Action, and Pedagogy: Teaching from the Heart.* New York: Peter Lang, 2004.

Eyre, R. M. *Stewardship of the Heart.* Houston: Ink, 1990.

Gibran, K. *The Prophet.* New York: Knopf, 1981.

Hall, B. "J." *Among Cultures: The Challenge of Communication* (2nd ed.). Belmont, Calif.: Thomson/Wadsworth, 2005.

Holy Bible: Authorized King James Version. Salt Lake City: Church of Jesus Christ of Latter-Day Saints, 1979.

Palmer, P. J. *The Courage to Teach: Exploring the Inner Landscape of a Teacher's Life.* San Francisco: Jossey-Bass, 2000.

Peck, M. S. *The Road Less Traveled.* New York: Simon & Schuster, 1978.

Schram, P. *Learning Wisdom from the Jewish Oral Tradition.* In D. Denton and W. Ashton (eds.), *Spirituality, Action, and Pedagogy: Teaching from the Heart.* New York: Peter Lang, 2004.

Schwehn, M. R. *Exiles from Eden: Religion and Academic Vocation in America.* Oxford, England: Oxford University Press, 1993.

BRADFORD "J" HALL is the head of the Department of Languages, Philosophy, and Speech Communication at Utah State University. His research focuses on issues of culture, identity, membership, conflict, and everyday conversation.

6

In this chapter, the author explains how teaching and interacting with American Culture and Language Program (ACLP) students allowed him to reconnect with his own Asian roots and gave him an opportunity to find his spirituality by confronting and celebrating Asianness in the hybrid public speaking classroom.

Finding Spirituality Through Confrontation and Celebration of Asianness in the Classroom

Richie Neil Hao

One September morning, I woke as a teacher—an international teaching assistant (ITA), to be exact—at a California State University (Cal State). As a twenty-five-year-old teaching assistant, I had the opportunity to teach hybrid public speaking classes that were designed for the American Culture and Language Program (ACLP), which turned out to be a spiritual awakening.

At least once a year, the Department of Communication Studies at Cal State works with the university's Division of Extended Education to facilitate a public speaking class for ACLP students. I was assigned to teach a hybrid ACLP public speaking section during the 2004 winter and fall quarters. Cal State is an urban university located east of Los Angeles, which enrolled 20,637 students in fall 2003. The school had 1,141, or 5.5 percent, international students. It is important to note that ACLP students are considered international students, but they are not the typical international students who get admitted through the university; instead, they enroll through the Division of Extended Education Program, which allows open enrollment to the public. At first, I did not know how I would facilitate this "special" class. My initial reaction was to change my curriculum. More important, I was worried about grading the speeches of ACLP students; I assumed that they might have difficulty communicating in English. To my surprise, having ACLP students in my class did not pose any significant challenges to me

NEW DIRECTIONS FOR TEACHING AND LEARNING, no. 120, Winter 2009   © Wiley Periodicals, Inc.
Published online in Wiley InterScience (www.interscience.wiley.com) • DOI: 10.1002/tl.376

47

as an instructor. The real challenge was my confrontation with Asianness in the classroom. For the first time, I was not concerned about whether or not my ACLP students would question my command of English, as I normally would in other non-ACLP public speaking sections. I felt some sense of belongingness with students who were just like me, at least ethnically speaking.

The particularity of this encounter forced me to revisit my own sense of projected otherness (as constructed by others) in the body and manner of my mostly Asian students. In this encounter, I came to understand otherness not exclusively as pathology but as a unique set of cultural cues that are most easily understood and respected by those who share those symbols and cultural practices in relation to those who mark them as different (Alexander, 1999). In many ways, teaching ACLP students led me to find my spirituality. To understand what I mean by "spirituality," I will use Kirkwood's definition: "an individual's or community's ultimate existential aspirations and the means of achieving these aspirations" (1994, p. 16). Kirkwood asserts that everyone has several aspirations, and one or more of these goals or motives promote "the highest, most perfected state of being. . . . These ultimate ends and the means believed to aid their attainment can be called 'spirituality'" (p. 16). Since I was in a classroom space where I reconnected and celebrated my Asianness with those who appreciated it, I felt that my state of being could not be better; it was an ideal place to be.

Asianness in the Classroom

Recognizing Asianness Through Lunar New Year. As Lunar New Year comes and goes every year (around the end of January or early February), I always announce in all of the classes I teach how important this holiday is to me and to various Asian communities, especially to the Chinese and Vietnamese. Although non-Asian students get a little excited that I would allow a potluck during the class period to celebrate the holiday, most of them do not understand what this holiday entails and why it should be celebrated. By contrast, my Asian ACLP students appreciate the actual meaning of the Lunar New Year. Perhaps they appreciate the fact that an aspect of Asian culture is being celebrated in the classroom, initiated by an Asian instructor. After my announcement of the Lunar New Year potluck, my ACLP students' eyes light up like kids receiving their favorite toys on Christmas morning, and their mouths are wide open, their teeth showing— signifying a feeling of joy and belongingness.

My decision to celebrate the Lunar New Year was immediate; I did not have to think twice whether or not I should do it in this specific hybrid classroom. After all, I never really experienced a day in school as a student where I felt I was important. Even though an Asian American month was often mentioned in schools I attended, there was nothing significant about this special month because it only made white people feel good about them-

NEW DIRECTIONS FOR TEACHING AND LEARNING • DOI: 10.1002/tl

selves celebrating "diversity," while ethnic minorities' experiences were ignored. As Spivak (1993) points out, the practice of Euro-American university education continues to teach us about white American history rather than our own individual experience. Because I did not want my ACLP students to go through what I did, I decided to go against the norm and celebrated the Lunar New Year.

On Lunar New Year 2004, I walked into the classroom wearing a red shirt and black pants in celebration of this holiday. In the Chinese culture, red is the color of good luck and fortune (Lum, 2006); therefore it was fitting to wear a red shirt on New Year's Day to bring happiness and wealth for the year. The Lunar New Year is like a "spiritual tradition" (Kirkwood, 1994, p. 17), a special holiday that united my ACLP students and me together as one. The Lunar New Year is one of many "spiritual traditions," which are "historical lineages of people who seek similar goals" (p. 17). Crocker-Lakness (2000) gives an example of spiritual tradition through New Age spiritualism, which values "communion, forgiveness, and a dual epistemology of language as both presentational and representational" (p. 123). Unfortunately, Crocker-Lakness states that certain traditions, such as New Age spiritualism, are often ignored thanks to their status of not being perceived as mainstream enough. The Lunar New Year allowed my students and me to celebrate something familiar to us.

When I entered the classroom, I saw a diverse representation of foods arranged on four desk chairs set horizontally in the middle of the room. Three of the four desks contained a variety of foods: cookies, chicken from a local chain, sushi rolls, chips, and donuts. The other table had drinks (all two-liter sodas), plastic spoons, forks, knives, paper cups, and napkins. Smiles were apparent on my ACLP students' faces, so I smiled back and greeted all of them by saying "Happy New Year" in three Chinese dialects: Cantonese (*kong hay fat choy*), Mandarin (*kong si fa tsai*), and Taiwanese (*kyong hi huat tsai*). After hearing me speak these three Chinese dialects, my ACLP students were amazed and perhaps appreciative of my efforts. After speaking Chinese, I asked my ACLP students how I did. Some of them responded verbally without hesitation with a big smile on their face: "Very good!" In a way, I was not sure how my Chinese was going to sound, because I hardly spoke most of these dialects. However, I felt that my ACLP students also accepted me as one of them. In a sense, these students considered me as part of their in-group, which aligned me as culturally similar to them (Appiah, 1996). To avoid excluding other students who did not speak Chinese, I also said "Happy Lunar New Year!"

As a teacher of two hybrid ACLP classes, I had to adapt the way I communicated to international students verbally and nonverbally. In particular, it was important to use language that was appropriate for ACLP students. Cazden, John, and Hymes (1972) address the importance of how language is used in the classroom as opposed to how language is structured. They argue that studying language should be focused on its use in different communities, because "features of intonation, tone of voice, rhythm, style" vary from one culture to another, which may convey "respect or disrespect,

concern or indifference, intimacy or distance, seriousness or play, etc."
(p. xiii). By greeting my ACLP students in Chinese dialects, I knew that it
would result in spiritual discourse between my students and me because I
showed that I cared about their cultural presence in the classroom. Kirkwood (1994) considers "spiritual discourse" as "those [exchanges] used to
enable ultimate states of being, as well as those that express someone's
understanding of what constitutes ultimate states of being" (p. 17). By
speaking in these dialects, my ACLP students saw it as an opportunity for
me to acknowledge that their Asian bodies did exist, which allowed me to
include their language, culture, and history. After all, Asian perspectives
are underrepresented in academia where students' Asianness is often
ignored. Much as in the classroom, Shimakawa (2002) explores the concepts of "Americanness" and "Asian Americanness" through drama and
performance art. Shimakawa argues that the forms of Asian Americanness
that are seen in U.S. culture are a national abjection, which is a process that
defines Americanness without the Asian American experience. In my classroom, intracultural representation existed where I, an Asian instructor, was
performing my Asian identity in front of my Asian students. This is also
why the Lunar New Year narrative was an important aspect of the classroom because I needed to reinforce that one's cultural experience or holiday should not be Americanized. Asian cultural practices and holidays
continue to be ignored by the mainstream U.S. American society, so Asian
Americans are essentially culturally invisible. In my own classroom, a way
to respond to the cultural invisibility of the Asian American experience
was to celebrate the Lunar New Year. By my doing so, my non-Asian students would at least recognize that Asian Americans exist and are as important as other ethnic groups, with their own particular set of customs,
practices, and beliefs.

A Taiwanese Conversation with Two ACLP Students. Two of my
ACLP students, Joan and Melissa, came to visit me one time during office
hours. They came to ask some questions about their group proposal speech.
After having an in-depth explanation of the assignment, Joan asked if I knew
how to speak Mandarin Chinese. I explained to them that I studied Mandarin
Chinese in the Philippines and in college in the United States, but I have not
spoken it that much since, so my Mandarin Chinese is "rusty." Then I asked
if they both knew how to speak Taiwanese, and they said "yes," with a smile.

Our conversation went on for about fifteen minutes, and in the process
I revealed my ethnic, linguistic, and cultural background to them by speaking in Taiwanese half of the time. In fact, I told them about my paternal and
maternal grandparents regarding where they came from and where my parents were born. Self-disclosure is not uncommon for teachers to share with
students. As a matter of fact, Cayanus (2004) claims that teachers "also talk
about themselves, tell stories, and share their personal beliefs. When these
behaviors occur, teachers are engaging in self-disclosure" (p. 6). With Joan
and Melissa, I voluntarily self-disclosed about my personal life because there

NEW DIRECTIONS FOR TEACHING AND LEARNING • DOI: 10.1002/tl

was an established ethnic identification and affinity between us, which was a kind of "spiritual experience"; the conversation was an experience "understood by someone, the experiencer or an observer, to be especially meaningful within the context of a given form of spirituality" (Kirkwood, 1994, p. 17). Overall, the conversation allowed us to free our Asianness in an office space to interact in a way that was difficult to do in a classroom representing Western ideals. In U.S. American classrooms, it is not unusual for teachers to not talk about Asian experiences. So my conversation with Joan and Melissa allowed us to revisit some of things we had in common.

Moreover, Cayanus claims that teacher self-disclosure is "related to students' likelihood to engage in out-of-class communication (e.g., talking with teachers during their office hours or in the hallway)" (2004, p. 7). Therefore it was not a surprise that Joan and Melissa disclosed some of the intimate details of where they came from, as well as aspects of their family life in Taiwan. As the conversation went on, I realized that both trusted me enough to share their personal narratives; it was comforting to get to know them as students. In addition to the perceived racial and cultural affinity, sharing our personal narratives with each other is perhaps why my ACLP students were more receptive to me than other students were. Also, language made it possible to communicate openly and comfortably through a specified system of cultural codes other than English.

Additionally, it can perhaps be explained that my ACLP students did not feel threatened thanks to the similarity of my ethnic identity with theirs. With this sense of ethnic identity, it is not surprising that these students did not resist my authority in the classroom. In particular, culturally, Asian students are taught to respect their teachers. As Liu (2001) indicates, students who come from high-power-distance Asian cultures are "expected to respect their teachers as authorities and accept what is taught without question" (p. 21). So even though my youthful appearance and age can pose a challenge to gaining recognition of teacher status from students in general, Asian students are taught to respect their teacher no matter what the age.

What sets ACLP students apart from other students is that they needed a lot of guidance and support; they had to make a major transition from their language-program classes to an actual college preparatory class. Therefore, it was necessary for me to make them feel they belonged in my classroom with other students. Perhaps spirituality is also about "finding a life's calling" (Bogart, 1994, p. 6) where it involves "the conscious holding of ultimate goals and the conscious effort to achieve these goals and help others to do so" (Kirkwood, 1994, p. 16). Having ACLP students in my class made me realize my life's calling to look after them like a guardian angel and make sure they will have a positive experience while attending an American university as international students.

The hybrid class also became an opportunity for my ACLP students to perform their Asianness freely because they knew that we both shared the same values in the classroom. Edwards and Harwood (2003) argue that individuals gain a part of their self-concept from the groups they identify with. As can be seen, Joan and Melissa were not hesitant to share their personal experiences with me during office hours. Having the same ethnic background and speaking the same language allowed Joan, Melissa, and me to establish our own individual self-concepts through our cultural membership.

Discussion: Becoming Visible

My ACLP students appreciated what I had to offer as a teacher. In ways that I clearly understood, I believe that my students saw aspects of themselves reflected in me as I did in them. These reflections were not just the physical markings of Asianness that can sometimes become reductive, as in "all Asians look alike." They saw and appreciated a cultural knowing or validation of their worldview through Asian eyes. Without overexaggerating the point, I believe that this was a spiritual moment. Teaching ACLP students was a spiritual moment because the whole experience was "profoundly enjoyable, as well as liberating or leading to salvation, freeing one from suffering and insecurity" (Kirkwood, 1994, p. 21). For the first time in a long time, I reclaimed my Asianness without the need to compromise who I was. My racialized Asian body was no longer invisible and was proudly to be marked as such.

Furthermore, the knowledge I gained from teaching ACLP students reveals that "we share not only the same basic needs, but indeed a fundamental identity and unity" (Kirkwood, 1994, p. 21). The classroom space we created was like a tight-knit community where we could be ourselves without worrying what others thought of us. Throughout the years of my own schooling, I never thought I could find a classroom moment in my hybrid ACLP classes where there was a tremendous amount of support for each other. Above all, it was a moment of resonance and recognition for all of us that allowed a unification of self, spirit, and soul. This might be a cornerstone in the meaningful interpersonal and intracultural relations that most definitely inform teaching, when the ethnic similarity between teacher and students helps to inform the educational enterprise.

My experience with teaching hybrid ACLP classes also taught me that I can serve as a mentor to students needing guidance and direction. My interaction with my ACLP students resulted in their getting to know me as an instructor who was willing to listen to their experiences of living in the United States and abroad. I remember how difficult it was for me growing up in the U.S. academy as an international student. I did not have anyone I could confide in and with whom to talk about the hardships I faced while acculturating into a new classroom environment. Unfortunately, I had to learn how to stand on my own two feet in order to survive the cultural and linguistic barriers I faced while starting out as an international student in the United States.

After reflecting on my own teaching experiences, I understood my ACLP students' difficulty in transitioning as international students, especially taking a college preparatory class with other students. After all, it is not easy to be in a foreign country, where one may experience anxiety not only in a public speaking classroom but also in the American academic culture at large. Fortunately, my ACLP students' fellow American peers and I were there for them. I suppose this was what made my hybrid ACLP classes so great. Everyone in each hybrid class was a part of a classroom family that they probably never experienced in other classes. As a result, my ACLP students, their peers, and I created a classroom space where we connected spiritually. Even though some of my "regular" students were not Asian, they appreciated the diversity ACLP students brought into the classroom. Therefore, all the students in each hybrid ACLP class collectively marked themselves as family (and perhaps even community).

Conclusion

Teaching is so rewarding, especially when students would tell me that they learned so much from my class. On some occasions, I received greeting cards from my students expressing their appreciation. The particular moment of receiving a thoughtful note from a student seems like icing on the cake. However, what is even more rewarding is when I get a chance to educate international students, as well as with ACLP students, because I can help them meet the challenges they may have to face while getting an education in the United States. More important, teaching ACLP students allowed me to find my spirituality by confronting and celebrating Asianness in the classroom. As an educator, at least I had the opportunity to finally acknowledge those who were marginalized because of racial, ethnic, cultural, or linguistic difference. By doing so, my ACLP students found my classroom to be a home away from home; they felt that they belonged there and that their cultural and racial identities were appreciated and celebrated.

As students, being able to identify with the teacher is an important aspect of what education is all about. It is our self-learning of who we are as individuals that will create a better understanding of how we are going to be represented in academia, even in society at large. Although I could not confront and celebrate my Asianness in the classroom as a student, I can finally do so as an educator. After all these years, my spirituality guides, sustains, and comforts me in this postsecondary setting to consciously perform my Asianness in a classroom space where I can finally feel both physically and spiritually alive.

References

Alexander, B. K. "Performing Culture in the Classroom: An Instruction (Auto)Ethnography." *Text and Performance Quarterly*, 1999, *19*, 307–331.

Appiah, K. A. "Identity: Political Not Cultural." In M. Garber, R. L. Walkowitz, and P. B. Franklin (eds.), *Fieldwork: Sites in Literary and Cultural Studies*. New York: Routledge, 1996.

Bogart, G. C. "Finding a Life's Calling." *Journal of Humanistic Psychology*, 1994, *34*, 6–37.

Cayanus, J. L. "Effective Instructional Practice: Using Teacher Self-Disclosure as an Instructional Tool." *Communication Teacher*, 2004, *18*, 6–9.

Cazden, C., John, V. P., and Hymes, D. *Functions of Language in the Classroom.* New York: Columbia University Press, 1972.

Crocker-Lakness, J. W. "New Age Spiritual Communication in *A Course in Miracles.*" *Journal of Communication and Religion*, 2000, *23*, 123–157.

Edwards, C., and Harwood, J. "Social Identity in the Classroom: An Examination of Age Identification Between Students and Instructors." *Communication Education*, 2003, *52*, 60–65.

Kirkwood, W. G. "Studying Communication About Spirituality and the Spiritual Consequences of Communication." *Journal of Communication and Religion*, 1994, *17*, 13–26.

Liu, J. *Asian Students' Classroom Communication Patterns in U.S. Universities.* Westport, Conn.: Ablex, 2001.

Lum, C.M.K. "Communicating Chinese Heritage in America: A Study of Bicultural Education Across Generations." In W. Leeds-Hurwitz (ed.), *Generation to Generation: Maintaining Cultural Identity over Time.* Cresskill, N.J.: Hampton Press, 2006.

Shimakawa, K. *National Abjection: The Asian American Body Onstage.* Durham, N.C.: Duke University Press, 2002.

Spivak, G. C. *Outside in the Teaching Machine.* New York: Routledge, 1993.

RICHIE NEIL HAO, Ph.D., is an assistant professor in the Department of Human Communication Studies at the University of Denver. His research interests are at the intersections of intercultural, pedagogical, and performance studies. He previously served as the assistant director of the core curriculum in the Department of Speech Communication at Southern Illinois University, Carbondale.

This autoethnographic chapter explores the thoughts, feelings, desires, and ethical struggles of the author when he rode along with a patrol officer and saw a dead body. Drawing on communication ethics, the author problematizes his ethics, faith, identity, and personal desires. He learns it is important for researchers to consider their personal ethical constitution while in the field.

The Most Exciting Thing: Researcher Ethics and Personal Ethics

Robert L. Ballard

> All bodies leave their mark. You cannot be near the newly dead without feeling it.
>
> —Nicholas Cage, "Frank Pierce,"
> *Bringing Out the Dead* (Scorsese, 1999)

A few years ago, at 1:00 a.m. on an April 1st, I was sitting in one of two patrol cars in a strip club parking lot. I was riding with a police officer, conducting an ethnography for my qualitative methods course. I didn't know it at the time, but on that chilly morning in a large urban city I would be experiencing the most exciting thing I'd see during my ride-alongs. Reflection on the events of that night demonstrates how what we study can affect the intellectual, ethical, emotional, and spiritual aspects of who we are as a person. This autoethnographic approach connects the personal and cultural by making me, the researcher, the subject (Ellis and Bochner, 2003).

Taking Bets on the Game

As we sat in the parking lot, the officers and I engaged in small talk about chicken wings, beer, and motorcycles. Over the police radio, we heard a fast, but conversational, interchange devoid of panic or worry. The female voice of the dispatcher on the radio said, "I've got a report of a pickup truck entering the off ramp of the interstate. Witnesses report the vehicle entered the

NEW DIRECTIONS FOR TEACHING AND LEARNING, no. 120, Winter 2009 © Wiley Periodicals, Inc.
Published online in Wiley InterScience (www.interscience.wiley.com) • DOI: 10.1002/tl.377

eastbound off-ramp and is now traveling westbound in the eastbound lane. Vicinity is just east of State Avenue. [short pause] Witnesses report single male driver of the pickup." Another officer piped in on the radio, this time a male: "Dispatch, this is [call number]. Do we have a more exact location?" The dispatcher responded, "Negative. Report came in less than two minutes ago," followed by the officer's response, "OK. I'll head en route."

In the car, I heard my officer say, "I bet he's DUI." The officer in the patrol car sitting next to us responded sarcastically, "Holy s$#@. What other kind?" My officer responded jokingly, "Oh f%$#, man. He's toast, I betcha." The other officer said, "No doubt. What a dumb f%$#." There were thirty seconds of silence in which we stared at the radio in anticipation. I glanced at the others and saw them also waiting to see what would happen next. Add in the chicken wings and beer we were talking about, and we could have been in a sports bar taking bets on whether or not our team would make the game-winning score. The dispatcher piped up again: "We have a report of an explosion and fire on the eastbound interstate just west of the State Avenue interchange. Would all nearby units please report. Emergency and fire services are en route."

My officer surprised me by shouting, "See what I told ya? He's f%$#@!% toast!" His response was surprising because, just like listening to a famous game-winning home run (or touchdown, or three-point shot), my officer's shout was one of celebration, like he won a bet and was gloating. And I, as one who'd never experienced listening to a fatality unfold on the radio, found myself caught up in the drama. I was a voyeur. But wait, isn't this a real person? Somehow, given the tenor of the conversation, I couldn't get there. I couldn't allow myself to be, as Emmanuel Levinas demands, "another for the others" (1998, p. 158); to see the dead body as a real person. In fact, I found myself thinking, "He gets what he deserves. What kind of moron gets drunk and drives west on an eastbound interstate?" It had to be a drama, the victim an objectified other, something not a person. If I began to care, I would see the other as a person, and if a person, I might not be able to deal with the situation if I were to go and see. And I wanted to go and see. I thought, *I want to go and see what happened.* And in the next instant, I thought, *Is it wrong to want excitement at the expense of a dead human being?*

My officer asked me, "Ever seen a burned body?" I responded, "No." He asked, "You want to see one?" An ethical moment came. I wanted to see the dead body. Not just because it would be a glimpse into the world of the police, but because I wanted to see one! It was not an ethical moment with society at stake, but an ethical moment with my personal narrative and identity at stake. What's important to me? What do I value? My response was, "Yes."

My officer told the other officer, "He's never seen a burned body so we're going to check it out." As we pulled out of the parking lot with lights flashing, he yelled excitedly, "Here we go! Carnage, man! Carnage!" Me? I was just trying to hold on as we ran through a red light, and caused all the vehicles around us to stop.

NEW DIRECTIONS FOR TEACHING AND LEARNING • DOI: 10.1002/tl

Faith

I believe in God. I have preached, taught in churches, and worked in ministry. Before entering my Ph.D. program, I spent a year in seminary considering whether or not I was called to ministry. I was not. Instead, I threw myself into social construction, phenomenology, and ethnography—paradigms that fly in the face of my traditional, evangelical teachings. But I love it. I see God in a whole new way. The church would classify me as postmodern, as someone who values relationship over rationality, community over individualism, stories over principles, dialogue over dogma, and paradox over logic. Fine. I'm not concerned with how I'm categorized. But now, more than any other time in my life, I have more faith.

With my research interests in communication ethics through ethnography, I am forced to look at my beliefs, and my examinations lead me to a stronger and deeper faith. Sometimes I do not have a rational or reasonable explanation for my faith, but I am learning to live in paradoxes and in uncertainty. As the Book of Hebrews states, "Now faith is being sure of what we hope for and certain of what we do not see" (Heb. 11:1, New International Version, or TNIV). Believing in something greater than myself is not a certainty, but faith is the retention of that belief when I experience uncertainty. My experiences force me to confront my faith and understand how frail and fragile I really am. I find myself thinking about who I am, mistakes I've made, people I've wronged, relationships I value, and accomplishments I'm proud of. Through my study of Levinas, I am becoming more attuned to my treatment of the other. As he writes, "The epiphany of the face is ethical" (1969, p. 199). For Levinas, when one encounters an-other, there is an ethical call that demands a response. I am learning to follow Jesus' command to "love thy neighbor as thyself" (Matt. 22:39, King James Version), to allow the other to demand my love and responsibility for them. As we headed toward the scene, I could sense I was going to be tested. Who am I? What do I believe? How will I respond?

Pig Flesh and the Call of Conscience

As we sped at more than a hundred miles an hour toward the crash, my thoughts were on what we would see when we came up to the fire and scene. "What's burning? How did the fire start? Were there more fatalities? What does a burned body look like? Will it smell? Will it still be in the truck? Will it gross me out? Will it give me nightmares?" In the short time it took to travel from the strip club parking lot to the scene of the accident, all of these thoughts ran through my mind. I left my persona as a researcher and became a voyeur, for how many people get to see an actual dead body? I was getting to see one, and I felt as if I would enter an elite club of some kind.

On the scene we encountered a burning pickup truck, a white semi truck with the front end smashed in, and a blue sedan with the windshield and cab area crumpled and a driver inside. Fire trucks, ambulances, and seven police officers were present. The driver of the sedan was still alive, but clearly in shock with wide eyes, dilated pupils, and white pale skin. Firefighters stood around the car examining how best to extricate him from the crumpled vehicle. The driver was conscious, and compared to the rest of the damage he was fortunate.

What struck me most about the scene was its finality and calm. There was no screaming, no crying, and no one calling out "Help!" Besides the fire, the chatter on the radio, and brief exchanges between emergency services personnel, the scene was strangely quiet and devoid of panic. There was no sense of urgency, even by emergency personnel extricating the driver.

The fire from the pickup cast light and heat on the scene. I was tempted to move toward the fire just to stay warm even though I knew there was a dead body in the cab of the burning pickup. The smell of burning flesh was in the air. My attempts at describing it fall far short of what it is actually like. It was a sickly, sweet smell, almost like barbecued pork. This should not be a surprise. But the difference is that pork causes me to feel hungry; this just caused me to feel sick.

The gas tank exploded twice while we were standing there. They were small explosions, and I was in no danger of being harmed, but I flinched anyway. Twice. I noticed that none of the emergency personnel or police officers flinched. I assumed that exploding gas tanks were not uncommon around burning vehicles. I prayed silently for my personal safety. I prayed that I would see my wife and family again. I don't know why exactly. Although I knew I was safe, I was uncomfortable. I wanted to feel that everything was OK. Was my anxiety from my concern over my physical safety, or my ethical struggle?

My officer and I conjectured that the pickup truck with the inebriated driver hit the blue sedan head on, then bounced off the sedan and crashed into the semi, where it exploded. After hitting the semi, the pickup spun 180 degrees and now faced the correct direction: eastbound. As I saw where the pickup truck was facing, I noticed the irony. The pickup driver was now facing the proper direction. Did he know he was driving in the wrong direction? Was this suicide, or an accident, or negligence? I began to consider my own mortality and think about my own family. I was thankful that my family was at home; it could easily have been them in the sedan.

Michael Hyde (2001) writes about the call of conscience in our lives. Building from Martin Heidegger and Emmanuel Levinas regarding ontology and ethics, Hyde claims that the call of conscience happens all the time: "We are bound to hear the call within the context of our everyday being-with-others" (p. 38). This call reminds us of our *"Dasein,"* or "the 'to be' of human existence" (p. 24). In my spiritual and religious system, Dasein is the gift of life, where God put the "breath of life" (Gen. 2:7, TNIV) into humanity. Put another way, the call of conscience is

A call whose saying is a showing, a revealing, a disclosing of our "potentiality-for-Being," of our "projective" involvement with the temporal process of becoming and understanding that which we are: our possibilities. The call of conscience, in other words, confronts us with the question of what it means to be [Hyde, 2001, p. 25].

When we are asked "How are you?" or "How are things going?" we consider the call of conscience in our lives. Hyde argues that in these moments we assess our Dasein, and we consider whether we live for ourselves or for others.

Here, standing just twenty feet from a burning body whose odor filled the air, I felt that call loud and clear. Hyde (2001) writes, "Human beings typically have a difficult time looking death in the face, and this difficulty is right before us when we are in the presence of those who remind us of our mortality and of how life can become a living death" (p. 261).

Standing so close to death, I realized how grateful I should be to have existence, to have relationships, and to be the one alive and not dead. Seeing the police officers and emergency personnel go about their duties, it struck me how unaffected they seemed to be by the tragedy. There was nothing I could contribute to the event, but there was a part of me, deep down, that thought I should learn something here, that this man's death should not be in vain.

But this call was subsumed by my desire to see the body. I felt guilty that I was going to be pleasured in seeing a dead and burned body. My conscience was calling. It was asking, "Are you not profiting personally and academically from this individual's fatal mistake?" It was asking, "Who are you?"

The Other?

As my officer took me over to the body, he used his flashlight to shine light onto the corpse sitting in the driver's seat of the pickup. I saw a white male (the right arm still had skin on it) with his head leaning back against the driver's seat and tilted to his left, almost resting on his left shoulder. The chest, neck, and head area looked like "BBQ chicken" (my description). Could this be because of the chicken wing conversation not fifteen minutes ago? I could see his teeth and nothing of his face. His face had been burned off; there was no nose, lips, or hair, and the eyes were closed. There was no way to recognize the person. From my untrained eye, I concluded that he was killed instantly. The body seemed to be at rest, like it was sleeping and would wake up at any moment. The corpse's left arm was hanging out the driver's side door opening (the door had been removed) and his right arm was sitting on the seat. I would think that someone who was realizing they were going to hit another car would bring his or her arms up to protect his face. I could not see his legs because of the steering wheel blocking the view.

While looking at the body, I kept telling myself, *This isn't a movie. This is real. It's a dead body. It's a former person.* Yet it felt like a movie. No, it's really just a situation that needs to be handled. It's another in a series of events the police handle. That isn't really a dead person. It's just evidence from a fatal accident.

I stared at the body for a few moments. My curiosity and desire held me. Interestingly, I had no affective reaction. I did not feel sad or angry, I did not feel relieved or elated, and I did not feel excited or panicked. I did not feel anything for the corpse. Nor did I feel any move to vomit. In fact, I found nothing gross about the experience at all, nothing physically disturbing about the experience of seeing a dead and burned body.

In my mind, I prayed for the victim and his family, but my heart wasn't really in it. It seemed like the right thing to do, a product of my past religious ritual. My conscience was calling me to see this corpse as a human. Instead of letting my experience of viewing death affect me, I said a rote prayer, hoping God would save me from my guilt.

As I walked back to the patrol car, I thought again, *He gets what he deserves.* In a moment when death called upon my conscience, I was more concerned with my own Dasein than with the history of the corpse, with the history of a person. I did not become "responsible for the evil in the other—for the evil that torments him as well as the evil he commits" (Levinas, 2001a, p. 55). Instead, I created distance by blaming the other for his mistakes. I believed I had done nothing to contribute to the death of this man, that it was entirely his fault. In short, I privileged my goals, my existence, my desires, and myself over this former person. I wondered, *What would God think? Am I doing what Jesus would do?*

Zygmunt Bauman (1993), who builds from Levinas, writes, "Ambivalence lies at the heart of morality . . . I am I in as far as I am for the Other" (p. 78). However, I might respond that God is the only being that is truly for the Other in everything. This is not how Western thought has traditionally regarded God, though. It is generally believed that God is the ontological ground of all morality, and morally universalistic principles are derived from God's ontological constitution. Said differently, God is the ultimate foundation on which morality and ethics are built. But if we take Bauman's assertion that "morality is before being" and that "the *moral* self can be no other than a moral *self*" (p. 75), then God is not an ontological foundation, but a subjective foundation. That is, God is first a subject, not first an immutable foundation.

God, and in my faith system Jesus as well, is the moral fulfillment. No other being can lay claim to the moral purity and holiness that characterize God. Because God is moral and holy, it is in the posture of *being* for others that constitutes God as *the* moral foundation. This is not a principalistic and propositional foundation, but a *relational* one. This claims that because God *is* for all others, God is morality. This is not ontology, but subjectivity. As moral beings we are not first ontological, fixed, certain, and essential. Rather, we are first relational agents by whose actions morality is constituted. This is not because of any universal or a priori givens, but because our choices and actions bring morality into being. We make choices as agents and subjects based on our sociality, on our relationships. God does the same (actually, we should say that we follow God's pattern of bringing morality into being). God makes choices based on his relationship to humanity, collectively and individually. But God's choices are always for the other, and in making those choices he constitutes himself and his relations as moral.

When I was gazing on the dead body, I was constituting myself and my morality as selfish and my relation to the dead person as objectifying. Caught up in the phenomenological world of the police, walking away from a dead body, a former person, generating internal dialogue that blamed this other, I separated myself from his humanity. I generated indifference and remoteness. I did not want to know who he was. I wanted to profit and pleasure, academically, personally, and professionally. He was dead to be sure, but as Levinas (1989) states, "The other man's death calls me into question . . . in doing so recalls my responsibility, and calls me into question" (p. 83). This death was asking, How ought I to respond? Should I respond by objectifying, or with compassion?

My evangelical teachings have led me to objectify. Note comments by Christian philosopher Douglas Groothuis (2000): "Apologists must be wary of working to make the Christian message relevant to the felt needs of non-Christians" (p. 163), or "We must dynamically engage the thinking of postmoderns" (p. 164). The terms apologists, Christian, non-Christian, and postmoderns objectify real human beings and reduce them to a collection of worldviews and moral categories, rather than considering an encounter with each person as a spiritual experience, or as though "the divinity of God is played out in the human" (Levinas, 2001b, p. 236). There is also the possibility that a "non-Christian postmodern" might not fit into the descriptions given in a well-meaning book. In short, we are taught to read others as objects, not as persons. My religion has taught and trained me to objectify first, not see how God might play out in the other. My time in seminary, Sunday school, and listening to sermons has taught me to see people as objects, categorized as Christian or non-Christian, believer or nonbeliever. I objectify others first, not move to care or be responsible for them first. Is this because of the teachings I have been exposed to, or simply my own experience? Probably a little bit of both, but there are many others who question whether or not evangelical teachings really teach us to love the person rather than objectify.

The greatest commandment, says Jesus, is to "love thy neighbor as thyself" (Matt. 22:39, King James Version). Jesus does not say to judge your neighbor or to categorize your neighbor first, but to love. Since completing my Ph.D. and studying thinkers such as Emmanuel Levinas, I have come to see that loving others is not about making sure someone believes as I do, but loving them as she or he is and taking the risk to enter a relationship with her or him. This is being for the other as God is. This is being for the other as Jesus was when he died on the cross.

NEW DIRECTIONS FOR TEACHING AND LEARNING • DOI: 10.1002/tl

In the moment where I gazed on the body of the dead other, of a dead person, my response was to objectify. I was justifying the dead person's behavior as the dead person's, as though I were morally superior, separated from his dastardly mistake. Most would suggest that my reaction was normal, that in the presence of the dead whom we do not know, it is normal to objectify. Possibly this is true, but in this case I'm not sure my "normalcy" is justified; maybe as an ethnographer and a person I should strive for more. Perhaps my first move should be to consider the dead body as a former person, not as an object.

Life-Giving Gift

As my officer and I drove away from the scene, a sense of compassion surfaced. I commented to my officer that the scene was a sad one. I was still unable to muster any emotion for the man in the pickup, but I felt that to let the experience pass without recognizing that the body was a former person was unethical. My officer said, "I hope there isn't a family waiting up for this guy." He had more compassion than I did for the dead man, but I agreed with his statement. I prayed again as I looked out the window into the early morning sky. This time I whispered it, not loud enough so my officer would hear, but so it was real. I prayed for his family and friends. I prayed someone would miss him and that the person would not be too sad. I still pray about that man and his family and friends.

Earlier I referenced Hyde as mentioning how "life can become a living death" (2001, p. 261). In *The Life-Giving Gift of Acknowledgment*, Hyde (2006) refers to this living death as social death, asking, "What would life be like if no one acknowledged your existence?" (p. 1) He develops the idea of how acknowledgment is a life-giving gift: "We need acknowledgment as much as we need such other easily taken for granted things as air, blood, and a beating heart" (p. xiv). But what about in death? What about after one has died? Wyatt (2005), in an autoethnographic story of his father's death, suggests, "to stop narrating stories is to cease being alive and I don't want him, or me, to die just yet" (p. 731). For Wyatt, his father still lived because his son was still telling his story; Wyatt continues to give the life-giving gift of acknowledgment even after death, even after the spirit has left the corporeal body.

Bauman (1993) says, "The moral call is thoroughly personal" (p. 60). Morality and ethics happen in relation to an-other. "It is in this creation of meaning of the Other, and thus also of myself, that my freedom, my ethical freedom, comes to be" (p. 86). In other words, how I respond to an-other is how my ethics are created, realized, and constituted. Understanding this, we can see how God is the ultimate moral and ethical constitution because God is always for the other, as exemplified in the sacrifice of his son (John 3:16, TNIV). I ask myself, then, How does my response to the dead other constitute my personal morality and ethics? Can we be deemed unethical in relation to a dead other while also being ethical to our occupational roles? Where is the line within one's self where one should seek a phenomenological lived experience and balance personal ethics of the treatment of the other? Where would God say that line is? Am I being moral? Do I live up to my spiritual standard? The Bible never answers these questions. Neither do Levinas or Heidegger.

At some point, in my role as a researcher, I needed to consider how my response to wanting to see the dead body and objectifying the dead body constituted a certain kind of communication ethics. I needed to stop merely being-with and being-near the body and take time being-for the other. As Hyde writes, "Being with others carries with it the obligation of *Being-for* others" (2001, p. 114). Maybe that moment was when we were driving away from the scene and commenting on the sadness of the situation. Maybe that moment is now, when I reflect on my Dasein and you read this to consider your own call of conscience.

Research, Spirituality, and the Call of Conscience

Denzin (1999) writes that ethnography is "a moral ethnography that reads repression and pain biographically, existentially. It knows that behind every act of institutional repression lurks a flesh and blood human being who can be held accountable at a deep, moral level, for his or her actions" (pp. 571–572).

Denzin points toward the centrality of ethics and morality in conducting ethnography. He also points to the underlying spiritual makeup of who we are as people. If this is so, then in the field we should feel Hyde's call of conscience on our lives. This can be a spiritual call, as it was for me, or it can be a call from our own unique social position and moral standards. Either way, it should call on our conduct as researchers as we consider our own Dasein and how we respond to others, dead or living.

The autoethnographic approach employed here allows me to explore the call of conscience on my own ontology, spirituality, and values while in a role as a researcher. It allows me to demonstrate the challenging and conflicting messages of my faith as they construct my personhood. The experience of seeing a dead body was as much about conducting ethnography as it was about who I am as a human being. I do not claim to be an impassive observer but claim to be affected by what I saw on that chilly night in April. It cut to my core as a person and my core as an ethnographer. It cut to the core of what I believe. It revealed how I am still influenced by past experiences in my religious system and the challenges I continue to face with my faith. It reveals how I am not fixed, but always moving, changing, and uncertain. It shows how far I need to go, and sometimes how little I care for others.

This chapter describes what it meant for one researcher to see a dead body and feel a call upon his life in ethical, spiritual, ontological, and epistemological ways. Here the reflexive considerations of the researcher are centralized in autoethnography. Here a dead body is the impetus for a spiritual experience. Here I intersperse a spiritual voice as a call on my conscience. Here is a glimpse of a dead body and how it places demands on who we are (our ontology) and forces us to consider what and who we value and why. I hope it spurs us on to value the other, whoever the other is, alive or dead, faithful or not, as worthy of acknowledgment, care, and ethical responsibility. If you come away seeing life just a little bit differently, then I will have fulfilled Denzin's call for a new ethics of writing that "demands that writers put their empirical materials in a form that readers can use in their own lives" (1999, p. 568). I learned something through the *most exciting thing I've seen* about what I value and how to respond. I've also learned how my responses have an impact on my ethics as a researcher and as a human being. What calls on your conscience?

References

Bauman, Z. *Postmodern Ethics*. Oxford: Blackwell, 1993.

Denzin, N. K. *Two-Stepping in the '90s. Qualitative Inquiry*, 1999, 5, 568–572.

Ellis, C., and Bochner, A. P. "Autoethnography, Personal Narrative, Reflexivity: Researcher as Subject." In N. K. Denzin and Y. S. Lincoln (eds.), *Collecting and Interpreting Qualitative Materials* (2nd ed.). Thousand Oaks, Calif.: Sage, 2003.

Groothuis, D. *Truth Decay: Defending Christianity Against the Challenges of Postmodernism*. Downers Grove, Ill.: InterVarsity Press, 2000.

Hyde, M. J. *The Call of Conscience: Heidegger and Levinas, Rhetoric and the Euthanasia Debate*. Columbia: University of South Carolina Press, 2001.

Hyde, M. J. *The Life-Giving Gift of Acknowledgment*. West Lafayette, Ind.: Purdue University Press, 2006.

Levinas, E. *Totality and Infinity: An Essay on Exteriority*. (A. Lingis, trans.). Pittsburgh, Pa.: Duquesne University Press, 1969. (Original work published in 1961)

Levinas, E. "Ethics as First Philosophy." In S. Hand (ed.), *The Levinas Reader*. Malden, Mass.: Blackwell, 1989. (Original work published in 1984)

Levinas, E. *Otherwise than Being, or, Beyond Essence*. (A. Lingis, trans.) Pittsburgh, Pa.: Duquesne University Press, 1998. (Original work published in 1974)

Levinas, E. "Interview with François Poirié." In J. Robbins (ed.), *Is It Righteous to Be? Interviews with Emmanuel Levinas*. Palo Alto, Calif.: Stanford University Press, 2001a. (Original interview in 1986)

Levinas, E. "On the Usefulness of Insomnia." In J. Robbins (ed.), *Is It Righteous to Be? Interviews with Emmanuel Levinas*. Palo Alto, Calif.: Stanford University Press, 2001b. (Original interview in 1994)

Scorsese, M. (prod., dir.). *Bringing Out the Dead* [Motion picture]. Hollywood, CA, United States: Paramount Pictures and Touchstone Pictures, 1999.

Wyatt, J. (2005). "A Gentle Going? An Authoethnographic Short Story." *Qualitative Inquiry*, 2005, 11, 724–732.

ROBERT L. BALLARD, Ph.D. is an assistant professor in the Communication, Leadership and Social Innovation Unit at the University of Waterloo, Ontario, Canada. He wrote this while a doctoral student in the Department of Human Communication Studies at the University of Denver, Colorado. His research focuses on communication ethics, especially through the thinking of Emmanuel Levinas, a 20th century French philosopher in the Continental tradition. He utilizes ethnographic and autoethnographic approaches in seeking to understand how communication constitutes ethics in our everyday experience.

NEW DIRECTIONS FOR TEACHING AND LEARNING • DOI: 10.1002/tl

SECTION THREE

Spirituality as Strength to Endure

Traditional Christian hymns and journal entries are intertwined to illustrate how the author's faith sustains and allows her to meet the challenges and triumphs of academia. Lyrics and excerpts from journal entries are the foundation for discussing obstacles, gratitude, and resilience as a black female in academia.

The Spirit That Strengthens Me: Merging the "Life of the Mind" with "Life in the Spirit"

Katherine Grace Hendrix

> The entanglements I experience in the classroom are often no more or less than the convolutions of my inner life.
> —Palmer (1998)

Traditionally, education and instructional communication scholars have called for reflective teaching—a time to review one's knowledge and ability to effectively communicate subject matter content to students. However, during the past decade, the notion of reflective teaching has been reconceptualized to incorporate reflection about one's persona, or presentation of the soul, in the classroom. For example, Orr (2005, p. 87) maintains, "Holistic education means that we strive to teach the whole person as a human soul which includes mind, body, emotions, and spirits" while her contemporary observes, "My concern is for the soul. Our current focus on facts and science and skills highlights a certain dimension of human reality but overlooks others. An emphasis on mind has generated neglect of soul" (Moore, 2005, p. 9). Moore believes that educating the soul means "teaching certain subjects and doing it in a way that brings the soul forward into our awareness and our list of priorities" (p. 10). For this reason, scholars now espouse the value of holistic teaching encompassing not only the mind but the soul. Advocates of holistic teaching argue that failing to understand and nurture

NEW DIRECTIONS FOR TEACHING AND LEARNING, no. 120, Winter 2009   © Wiley Periodicals, Inc.
Published online in Wiley InterScience (www.interscience.wiley.com) • DOI: 10.1002/tl.378

human wholeness leads to fractured, unhappy, unhealthy, and unproductive lives.

When discussing the need for a holistic classroom approach, most of the literature mentions the importance of addressing the needs of one's soul. However, at least two perspectives exist regarding the soul. First, the metaphor of an animal is used. In this case, the soul is described as "tough, resilient, self-sufficient," with the ability to survive in hard places while simultaneously being shy, thus "seeking safety in the dense underbrush like a wild animal" (Palmer, 2004, p. 58). Second, in contrast to viewing the soul as an astute beast, in a religious context the soul is viewed as a hidden form of wholeness

> because otherwise it would become common and mundane . . . [so] God hides the Divine self so that we do not misuse God. What is hidden can be known if we have the right eyes for seeing. . . . Mystics see the hidden, because their eyes are cleansed [Dash, Jackson, & Rasor, 1997, p. vii].

Thus, in this latter case, the soul and the notion of wholeness are not connected to a soul/spirit that hides away in a bush but rather are part of a larger picture withheld from us by God until we are able to properly see and interpret the situation.

Wholeness brings to mind the soul/spirit and, quite naturally, a discussion of what constitutes spirituality. In general, the definition of spirituality is associated with an attitude or way of life that may or may not be connected to Christian, Buddhist, Hindi, Jewish, or Muslim religions. Whether the approach to the topic is religious or secular, the need to improve not only one's individual condition but one's community and society is a common theme. Of particular interest is the belief of Dash and colleagues (1997) that the unique experiences (slavery and discrimination) of African Americans "who have encountered a God who sustains and liberates . . . [has the potential to offer] the larger Western society a fresh and enriching spirituality unexperienced by far too many European Americans" (pp. 11–12).

Dash and colleagues duly note that African American spirituality fosters joys and gaiety even in the midst of heartache and therefore may be the type of spirituality needed in a world torn apart with great human suffering. Given my awareness of how spirituality affects my daily personal and professional interactions as a woman of color, working in a profession that remains predominantly white, and acknowledging the generally strong religious beliefs of people of color, I will briefly explore my lived experience as a female professor of color guided by faith in a higher power. First, I combine the use of traditional Christian hymns with a set of eclectic journal entries to God in order to reveal how the spirit strengthens me, thereby making me a better person, teacher, researcher, administrator, and academician in general. Second, I more directly discuss the role of prayer and a relationship with God as a foundation in handling the joys and demands of academia.

NEW DIRECTIONS FOR TEACHING AND LEARNING • DOI: 10.1002/tl

Rock of Ages: Home Training

> Rock of ages, cleft for me, Let me hide myself in Thee; Let the
> water and the blood, From Thy wounded side which flowed, Be
> of sin the double cure, Save from wrath and make me pure.
> —Morgan (2003, p. 74)

My parents, Samuel and Lizzie Grace, are very devout Christians. I recall spending many an evening, during my youth, sitting in the back of Deliverance Temple Nondenominational Church doing my homework while night service was conducted. The church was on a country road in the San Joaquin Valley of California, where the fog settles in so densely on winter nights you can barely see a foot in front of your car, but there we would be on Wednesday and Friday nights in prayer service; fog was not an acceptable excuse for missing the opportunity to "testify" about how good God had been, joyfully praising God, offering prayers for others, and requesting prayer for oneself and loved ones.

Christian biblical scripture says to train a child and she will not stray too far—or if she chooses to stray, she will not be doing so out of ignorance because she will certainly know better (Proverbs 22:6, New International Bible), so my faith sustains me through both the good and bad times. Amidst today's intermittent controversies regarding religion in the classroom (O'Neil and Loschert, 2002; Yen, 2005), I cannot fathom what kind of person and teacher I would be without my faith. My religious background provides the strength I need to address the challenges of being a black female professor in a still predominantly white profession (postsecondary teaching) and discipline (communication) and a society still ravaged by racism.

Academia is both rewarding and challenging, and I use this broader term, academia, to refer to the levels one experiences within postsecondary education: the classroom; exchanges with colleagues at the department, college, and campus levels; interaction with administrators; and disciplinary interchange such as conferences and publications. Just as some Christians believe in three heavens and others believe in intermediary stages between heaven and hell, within academia you can find yourself situated somewhere between heaven and hell or continually moving between heaven and hell (sometimes in the same day!) depending on the particular segments of academia in which you operate during the course of a day.

I Need Thee, Every Hour I Need Thee

> I need Thee, O I need Thee; Every hour I need Thee; O bless me
> now, my Savior, I come to Thee.
> —CME Commission on Hymnal (1987, p. 229)

NEW DIRECTIONS FOR TEACHING AND LEARNING • DOI: 10.1002/tl

Every day I pray about the known and unknown, the expected and unexpected. Basically, in addition to petitions on behalf of my family, I ask for strength and insight to get through my day—including my teaching day. Who would not need help when saying, "No, you cannot join the class four weeks into the semester" or "No, you are not getting out early so you can watch the game"? Below are several journal entries reflecting circumstances in my academic life that required spiritual help.

"I Need Thee" Journal Entries

Journal Entry, Fall 1994.
　　Lord, guess what happened to me today? One of my colleagues told a teaching assistant she didn't see any reason the graduate teaching assistants (GTAs) should have homework assignments or be required to complete teaching journals. Lord, you know this is my first year here and I don't have tenure. Help me to stand my ground.

Journal Entry, Spring 1996.
　　God, I received a rejection notice today. You knew it was coming and you also know how badly I need a publication. Let your will be done. [Silent thought: God, help me out here. I'm dying. You know that I must earn tenure. I don't want to have to move my family.]

Journal Entry, Fall 1996.
　　It is the first day of class and I just finished whipping my previous semester's students into shape and now it is time to start the process all over again. Why me, Lord? I guess it's the nature of the beast (academia). Oh, Lord. I have a problem and I need your help. I have heard through the grapevine that several GTAs are talking behind my back. It seems that several of them have an issue with me using our discussions from the GTA sessions as research data. As I understand it, these are some of the same GTAs who have spent hours in my office seeking counsel as they have faced serious challenges to their classroom authority and grading assessments. Why is it, Lord, that they think nothing of my White colleagues incorporating the themes from class discussion (Heck, even ideas from graduate student papers) into their research but these students murmur behind my back when I have asked their permission to use themes from our GTA meetings?

Journal Entry, Fall 1997.
　　Lord, I've met the requirements for full graduate faculty status but, of course, tenure is far more important. Give me the strength to swallow my pride and accept my application's rejection though my colleagues have accepted someone else's petition knowing full well that I also meet the qualifications. Let me hold my peace and fight this battle another time. As a Black person, I've dealt

with this double standard all my life (well, Lord, *you and I* have dealt with this double standard), so this looks like the usual thing—I will need twice the normal requirements before my application will be accepted. So, what else is new?

Thank You, Lord

> Praise God from whom all blessings flow; Praise Him all creatures here below; Praise Him above ye heav'nly host; Praise Father, Son, and Holy Ghost.
>
> —Morgan (2003, p. 20)

Just as I have faced many challenges in academia, I have also grown tremendously from a series of lessons that, at this stage in my life, necessitate giving words of thanks. There are plenty of times when I am blessed to be able to say, "I'd love to go out to dinner with you and your parents," "You've just completed your first year as an assistant professor with great evaluations; I'm so proud of you," and "Great! I want to host the baby shower." Every now and then, I even get to say, "Thank you so much for this lovely gift!" A few journal entries reflect my gratefulness for negative situations being turned into positive ones and for some circumstances where the news has simply been good from beginning to end.

"Thank You, Lord" Journal Entries

Journal Entry, Spring 1984.
    Do you remember, Lord, when I was teaching at Fresno City College as a relatively new instructor and when I passed back the first exam in one class, a White male about 10 years older than me, jumped up from his seat and scowled at me about his grade? I was simultaneously shocked, furious, and afraid. You have taught me many lessons so I might help other young teachers—especially GTAs and professors of color—and I thank you for the insights I have gained. He thought he could scream at a young, Black female and, thereby, discredit me for the rest of the semester while also intimidating me into a grade. You gave me the strength to stand my ground, keep control of my class, and maintain my authority.

Journal Entry, Fall 1985.
    Oh, God! What about that time when I began teaching at the community college level and had a student in the class who was old enough to be my Mom? I can't recall her name but I do recall my hesitation as I called out the class roll, "Bill, Susie, Lacey, Jamella, Mrs. Jones, Theresa, Juan. . . ." There I was again on the verge of tears as I sat face-to-face with her hoping she wouldn't mind if I used her first name. Thank you for getting me through that situation as well.

NEW DIRECTIONS FOR TEACHING AND LEARNING • DOI: 10.1002/tl

Journal Entry, Spring 1994.

Lord, thank you for sending me mentors at the different levels within academia. Mentors who respected me, acknowledged my intelligence, cultivated my success, and who helped me to navigate the minefields in my department and discipline.

Journal Entry, Summer 2000.

Thank you, Lord, for allowing me to mentor novice male and female teachers of all races, ages, and nationalities. Thank you for guiding me in bolstering the confidence of international GTAs of color, advising very young GTAs, and encouraging female teachers when others attempt to intimidate and discredit them. I also thank you for giving me the mind to acknowledge the presence and contributions of our adjunct faculty. Contrary to how they are often treated, the adjuncts are not invisible to me.

Journal Entry, Spring 2002.

Thank you, Lord, for my teaching award. I've always wanted one and have always known that I deserved one. I work so hard to know my content, teach well, show pride in my profession, and transfer my knowledge to others. It's been a long time coming but I'm so happy now.

Lord, do you remember my early teaching days as a graduate assistant? I was at UC Davis and trained under a young assistant professor, Elizabeth Mechling. She was young but excellent in the classroom and, as a result, I received a solid foundation for my independent teaching. I recall that the female faculty were few in number and experiencing some difficulties in the department but I was so focused on earning my M.A. degree and my new teaching responsibilities that I didn't pay much attention to their problems. I don't recall any problems as a TA at Davis though being a Black graduate student (or Black undergrad) was not really the norm during that time. I thank you for shielding me from classroom prejudices (or allowing any bad memories to stay buried!) during my time as a very young TA.

I Shall Not Be Moved

> To ole Hell asail me, I shall not be moved; Jesus will not fail me, I shall not be moved; Just like a tree that's planted by the water, I shall not be moved.
> —CME Commission on Hymnal (1987)

Whether the approach to the topic is religious or secular, the need to improve not only one's individual condition but one's community or society is a common theme in spirituality literature. The need to build relationships, remove unjust social systems, and, in regard to our teaching, cultivate serenity and compassion is a common topic among the consulted sources.

NEW DIRECTIONS FOR TEACHING AND LEARNING • DOI: 10.1002/tl

In fact, Orr (2005) discusses the need for antioppressive pedagogy as a means for "unlearning sexism, racism, classism, homophobia, religious intolerance, ableism, and other forms of discrimination" (p. 96).

To build relationships, Palmer (2004) offers "circles of truth" as a viable means for healing wounds received from living a divided life. Circles of truth allow participants to restore a sense of self in a supportive environment, thereby simultaneously restoring one's ability to discern and fulfill the spiritual needs of others. Related to the concept of circles of trust, Dash, Jackson, and Rasor (1997) say that spirituality should drive us to build relationships and "God invites us to find God not only in all of life's circumstances and situations, but also in community and with others" (p. 51).

After returning to graduate school and earning my doctorate in 1994, I entered a new phase of my career, moving from community college administrator and instructor into the role of university assistant professor. At the University of Memphis, I joined an interdisciplinary writing circle consisting of five women, four of whom stayed with the university and earned promotion to associate with tenure. We trusted each other with the trials and tribulations of our life as women in academia, and we combined "girl talk" with offering feedback on our research manuscripts. We even occasionally discussed issues associated with race and gender, but this group never discussed our spiritual or religious beliefs. Consequently, I sought spiritual affirmation and feedback specific to my discipline from yet another group. My actual circle of trust consisted of a group of six black female communication professors, specifically, five junior professors mentored by a senior professor, Marsha Houston, PhD. I could relate to the members of this second circle as women, black women, friends, and professional colleagues while also depending on them to nourish my spirit, and I often thanked the Lord for sending them to me.

There are so many challenges in academia, and as professors our responsibility to our students, colleagues, and community is great. I found spiritual support in communion with my husband, my family, and also within this circle of trust. When engaging in the scholarship of learning while teaching adolescent students, Kessler (2005) discovered seven areas of spiritual development: (1) searching for meaning and purpose, (2) longing for solitude and silence, (3) urging for transcendence, (4) hungering for joy and delight, (5) developing creative drive, (6) calling for initiation, and (7) forming a deep connection. In the last case, Kessler meant "connecting deeply to nature, to their lineage, or to a higher power" (p. 105). For me, the deep connection is a Christian foundation, but it doesn't necessarily have to be Christian. Whether your spiritual beliefs are grounded in religion or your standpoint is more secular, I suggest that you combine the "life of the mind" with life in the spirit.

Miller believes "our culture and educational systems have become obsessed with acquisition and achievement" (2005, p. 1), and as a result society is more interested in developing what Hillman (1999) dubbed the "objective observer" rather than educating the whole person. Of course, there is the quagmire associated with how much of ourselves to reveal to our students. I share my spiritual grounding not by proselytizing but rather by allowing my human frailties and humanity to come forth as I teach. In addition, I engage my best effort to maintain consistency between behavior in my private and professional life. What my students see in the classroom is very close to what they will see at the grocery store, at the movies, or in church service. I desire that my general behavior and treatment of others be a testimony to the spirit within. No fervent religious tirades or debates should be necessary; leading by precept is the key. This idea is consistent with Lillian Bowles's song "This Little Light of Mine":

> This little light of mine, I'm going to let it shine. Oh, this lit-
> tle light of mine,
> I'm going to let it shine. Hallelujah. This little light of mine,
> I'm going to let it shine;
> Let it shine, let it shine, let it shine; Ev'ry where I go, I'm going
> to let it shine.
> Oh, ev'ry where I go, I'm going to let it shine. Hallelujah. Ev'ry
> where I go,
> I'm going to let it shine. Let it shine, let it shine, let it shine.
> —CME Commission on Hymnal (1987, p. 401)

Epilogue: Leaning on the Everlasting Arms

Given the triumphs and trials of teaching, what allows my little light to shine? How do I handle the joys and demands of academia? Prayer is an integral part of my daily existence, allowing me to draw on and reflect (by no means am I perfect, which also accounts for the need for daily reflection and prayer) the spirit within me. Though God's form is unseen, He is not unknown to me. He guides me and talks to me as I read the Holy Bible, meditate, and pray. The Holy Spirit within me and the Word of God inform me of the importance of wholeness and yielding the fruits of the spirit— love, joy, peace, patience, kindness, goodness, faithfulness, gentleness, and self-control (Galatians 5:22–24). It is with this sense of wholeness, integrity, and sharing that I constantly strive to enter into the academic setting, thereby merging the life of the mind with the life in the spirit.

Wilkinson (2001) would refer to my conversations with God as "abid- ing" with Him. Just as a friendship (including parent and child) is nurtured by time spent together and mutual respect yielding knowledge of one another, so is the case with my relationship with God. I have matured enough that He can be not only Father but friend. As a matter of fact, I can see myself in the back row of hard, red, wooden theater chairs, the kind that are connected by wrought iron, where the seats fold up into the back of the chair to allow people to pass through the row. These seats were probably purchased or salvaged from an old fifties movie theatre in the process of being remodeled. At any rate, there I am doing my homework while Sister

NEW DIRECTIONS FOR TEACHING AND LEARNING • DOI: 10.1002/tl

Beatrice Webster leads the congregation in a song. I can hear her now. Listen. She's been singing *a cappella* and will soon bring in the tambourine. Let's listen in as she proudly opens testimony service by singing:

> What a fellowship, what a joy divine. Leaning on the everlasting arms. What a blessedness. What a peace is mine. Leaning on the everlasting arms. Leaning, leaning. Safe and secure from all alarms. Leaning, leaning. Leaning on the everlasting arms [Morgan, 2003, p. 218].

References

CME Commission on Hymnal. *The Hymnal of the Christian Methodist Episcopal Church.* Memphis, Tenn.: CME, 1987.

Dash, M.I.N., Jackson, J., and Rasor, S. C. *Hidden Wholeness: An African-American Spirituality for Individuals and Communities.* Cleveland, Ohio: United Church Press, 1997.

Hillman, J. *The Force of Character and the Lasting Life.* New York: Random House, 1999.

Kessler, R. "Nourishing Adolescents' Spirituality." In J. P. Miller, S. Karsten, D. Denton, D. Orr, and I. C. Kates (eds.), *Holistic Learning and Spirituality in Education: Breaking New Ground.* Albany: SUNY Press, 2005.

Miller, J. P. *"Introduction: Holistic Learning."* In J. P. Miller, S. Karsten, D. Denton, D. Orr, and I. C. Kates, (eds.), *Holistic Learning and Spirituality in Education: Breaking New Ground.* Albany: SUNY Press, 2005.

Moore, T. "Educating for the Soul." In J. P. Miller, S. Karsten, D. Denton, D. Orr, and I. C. Kates, (eds.), *Holistic Learning and Spirituality in Education: Breaking New Ground.* Albany: SUNY Press, 2005.

Morgan, R. J. *Then Sings My Soul: 150 of the World's Greatest Hymn Stories.* Nashville, Tenn.: Thomas Nelson, 2003.

O'Neil, J., and Loschert, K. "Navigating Religion in the Classroom." *National Education Association,* Nov. 2002. Retrieved June 29, 2005, from http://www.nea.org/neatoday/0211/cover.html.

Orr, D. "Minding the Soul in Education: Conceptualizing and Teaching the Whole Person." In J. P. Miller, S. Karsten, D. Denton, D. Orr, and I. C. Kates (eds.), *Holistic Learning and Spirituality in Education: Breaking New Ground.* Albany: SUNY Press, 2005.

Palmer, P. J. *The Courage to Teach: Exploring the Inner Landscape of a Teacher's Life.* San Francisco: Jossey-Bass, 1998.

Palmer, P. J. *A Hidden Wholeness: The Journey Toward an Undivided Life.* San Francisco: Jossey-Bass, 2004.

Wilkinson, B. *Secrets of the Vine: Breaking Through to Abundance.* Sisters, Ore.: Multnomah, 2001.

Yen, H. "No End for Church-State Tiffs." *Seattle Times,* June 29, 2005. Retrieved June 30, 2005, from http://seattletimes.nwsource.com/html/nationworld/2002351522_scotus29.html.

KATHERINE GRACE HENDRIX *is an associate professor in the Communication Department at the University of Memphis. She is an instructional communication scholar with an interest in the pedagogical contributions of and credibility challenges faced by professors and graduate teaching assistants of color, including international graduate teaching assistants with English as a second language. She also employs a critical approach to investigating implicit rules and issues of power associated with questions of epistemology, axiology, and ontology coupled with the academic research process and has published in journals and edited books.*

NEW DIRECTIONS FOR TEACHING AND LEARNING • DOI: 10.1002/tl

9

This chapter reflects on the shared journey of two African American women pursuing Ph.D.s, with a spiritual commitment to walk by faith. Afrocentric philosophy, communicative practices, and spiritually grounded pedagogical approaches to teaching and learning are examined in their transition from graduate students to university professors.

Spirituality Then and Now: Our Journey Through Higher Education as Women of Faith

Audrey M. Wilson Allison, Patreece R. Boone Broadus

Throughout a ten-year friendship and professional relationship emerging from a shared graduate school experience, we, the authors, have consistently acknowledged our spiritual beliefs as the fiber of our existence and purpose. Even though there are many occurrences in our personal lives from which we could each "testify" about the grace of God, we seek to focus on our shared religious tradition and its influence on our journey through academe, from doctoral students to university professors. Specifically, we examine reliance on spiritual convictions that uplifted, motivated, and energized us through the rigors of graduate study. This chapter explores how spirituality, infused with cultural identity, influences our current pedagogy.

Although the concepts of religion and spirituality are closely aligned and thus often used interchangeably, they are two distinct concepts. Religion is categorized as an external discipline or experience, a system or organization of practices such as rites and rituals that may be reflective of one's spiritual beliefs. Derived from the Latin word *religio*, meaning "good faith ritual," religion "involves universal life experiences and the meaning attached to these experiences" (Belgrave and Allison, 2006, p. 184). By comparison, spirituality, as a more elusive construct, is perhaps more challenging to define than religion. Spirituality is an internal way of knowing and holistic way of being, as "a major organizing principle in our lives" (Lauzon, 2001, p. 4). A belief in something or someone greater than oneself and

a sense of connectedness are prominent definitive views of spirituality (Mattis, 2002; Steingard, 2005). Spirituality reflects "wholeness" or centeredness, which Mattis describes as a "necessary condition for learning and growth" (2002, p. 313). As young female educators, we approached our academic endeavor with a spiritual vow to walk by faith, not by sight (II Cor. 5:7). Henceforth, the insight and experiences we now share are still rooted in the standpoint that our spirituality—and how deeply we embrace it—shapes and guides our lives.

Spirituality Then: Graduate Students

In a recent article, Delbecq (2004) credits the religious traditions of a calling (that is, mission or vocation) and spiritual friendship as the key factors in forming his identity and life as an educator/scholar. It is his perspective regarding spiritual friendship that is particularly pertinent to this discussion. Citing a quote from H. S. Skovoroda's *Salvation as Happiness: Thoughts by the Itinerant Ukrainian Philosopher Theologian, 1722–1794*, the author writes:

> Even high-quality friendships are chosen not by us but by a higher directive. . . . And just as congeniality to a vocation, so also an inclination to a friendship is obtained neither by buying, nor by asking, nor by force. But both are gifts of the Holy Spirit who divides everything according to His good will [Skovoroda, as cited in Delbecq, 2004, p. 625].

Just as Delbecq contends that his professional collaboration or friendships with colleagues were not guided by mere fate or chance but instead guided by God, we too acknowledge God's presence in the development of our relationship as graduate school classmates and close friends.

Crossing Paths: The Meeting. In the fall of 1995, we both were accepted into the doctoral program at a large Midwestern university. Although our paths were quite different, our simultaneous arrival at the university was, in our opinion, due to divine intervention. Audrey's original goal was to attend graduate school in a major city that offered more corporate opportunities. Thus a grad school program located in a small college town was not high on the list.

Audrey writes:

> As a young professional, I was quite pleased with my occupation as a shopping center marketing director. It was in fact, my dream job. Surprisingly, it synthesized all of the different business areas that interested me (marketing, PR, advertising, retail merchandising, and facility management). I thrived in this role, enjoying the variety of responsibilities and the creative freedom. I believe that there is a joyous sense of freedom in doing the kind of work you really want to do, the way you want to do it. This is what I truly value as my

"success." While others might attribute such an accomplishment to an advanced degree and a master's thesis on shopping center marketing, I acknowledged and praised God for bringing it to fruition.

While I enjoyed working as a marketing director, the invitation to teach part-time was also a blessing. I appreciated returning to a collegiate environment as a teacher. The intrinsic satisfaction I felt as an instructor prompted a new career interest. As I began contemplating leaving the corporate sector for full-time doctoral study, I had to pray. Before beginning the application process, before visiting schools, before charting the path, I knew it had to be a spiritual decision. I was going to exit a career experience that was fulfilling and promising. The transition to a new and challenging role as an "academic" would require four more years of graduate study . . . at least four. I thought, "HE has already done so much for me and yet, I am asking for more." I reaffirmed my belief that God could do exceeding abundantly above all that I could think or ask, according to the spiritual power that worked in me [Eph. 3:20, King James Version]. With continued prayer came confirmation. The spirituality that empowered me as a young African American professional would now empower me as a doctoral student. After visiting different campuses and talking particularly to African American faculty and administrators, I was convinced to return to my "home campus" for doctoral study. I believed it was my destiny to be there. Based upon the goodness-of-fit with my new academic goals and the warm campus environment, my spirit said "yes."

Audrey gave much thought to career advancement and the pursuit of graduate study for well over a year; Patreece, on the other hand, had no immediate intentions whatsoever to return to graduate school.

Patreece writes:

Reflecting upon my path toward the Ph.D. and a career in higher education, I am utterly convinced in my spirit that God led me to teach. Proverbs 16:9 (New International Version) states, "In his heart a man plans his course, but the Lord determines his steps." For me, the idea of leaving my (then) current teaching position to enroll in a Ph.D. program was certainly not at the top of my to-do list. Only after a colleague (who was an ordained minister) read about a fellowship opportunity in *The Chronicle of Higher Education* and urged me to apply, did I seriously consider pursuing a doctoral degree. As a result of this experience, I believed I could grow and mature as an educator, and be of greater value and service to my students. Equipped with a Ph.D., perhaps I could help my students to reach within themselves, to challenge and shatter stereotypical images either they or our society held of them (as ill-educated black students from the rural South), and accomplish their educational goals. Surely, I felt confident that this was what God was directing me to do. So with much prayer and pain, I quickly left my job at this small

Mississippi HBCU [historically black college or university] to become a full-time student once again.

From the concept of a "spiritual friendship" as mentioned by Delbecq (2004), we know our meeting at the same university was not by chance. This became more apparent as we later learned that we were recipients of two, out of only five, one-time university fellowships. Our belief in a shared destiny solidified when a graduate dean informed us that our academic department was initially reluctant to accept two fellowship awardees. When we reflect on these occurrences, Jeremiah 29:11 comes to mind: "for I know the plans I have for you" declares the Lord, "plans to prosper you and not to harm you, plans to give you hope and a future" (NIV). Thus the common denominator in this unexpected alignment of purpose between two grad students is the work of divine intervention. We therefore approach our friendship as a spiritual gift.

The Motto. To cope with conflicting emotions and adversities, we drew closer to our spiritual foundation. During one of our many late-night discussions, we recalled the words of Philippians 4:13: "I can do all things through Christ who strengthens me" (NKJV).

We also discovered another aspect of this shared insight: a direct connection between our cultural and spiritual identities. In her exploration of identity and black women's language usage, Scott (2004) examines the use of the terms *girl* and *look* as discourse markers in black women's speech among African American women attending a predominantly white university. She concludes that their use of *girl* serves as a marker of identity and solidarity "with other black women whom they perceive as sharing that same identity, and an understanding of that identity" (p. 172). Proclamations we shared such as "Girl, we can make it!" served as both a cultural marker of shared cultural identity and a spiritual affirmation of faith and purpose.

It is the concept of faith that brought clarity to our purpose. Faith is an undeniable trust in things hoped for and certainty of things yet to be seen. We believed it was God's plan for us to succeed academically. Although we experienced many challenges throughout our matriculation, embracing this scripture about faith (Phil. 4:13) encouraged us. We refused to be conquered by self-doubt, naysayers, racial bias, funding woes, physical exhaustion, or a tremendous load of teaching, research, writing, and so on. We relied on faith and spiritual conviction to guide us through graduate study. We applied the scripture's notation of "all things," literally and liberally, from course selection, preliminary exams, and prospectus to the dissertation defense and faculty job search. These milestones required critical preparation, but fulfillment of them was deemed so by our faith. Having walked by faith through the doctoral program, how would we use this same spiritual focus as teachers in our own classrooms?

NEW DIRECTIONS FOR TEACHING AND LEARNING • DOI: 10.1002/tl

Spirituality Now: The Teachers

Under the philosophy of political correctness and the "scrutinizing reward structure" of academe, many educators advocating or practicing spiritually infused pedagogy are often told to leave their religion outside the institutional doors (Dillard, Abdur-Rashid, and Tyson, 2000). If the concept of spirituality is subsumed under this line of thought, we then find ourselves challenging such an idea and questioning it, in both theory and practice. Simply stated, how are educators expected to abandon spiritual principles that ground a holistic teaching approach, or that are conceptually linked to his or her (cultural) identity? The literature offers a variety of dimensions for spirituality, in relation to truth and learning. Oladele states that "spirit is at the heart of a meaningful education" (1998–99, p. 62). Some of the common premises of spirituality within education emphasize self-identity, language and communication, and positive affirmation.

Spirituality and an Afrocentric Identity. On our present journey as educators, we have come to recognize and acknowledge the influence an Afrocentric perspective has on our spirituality, identity, and ultimately our mission as teachers. Forwarded by the works of Molefi Asante (1987, 1991), Afrocentricity is a frame of reference that places African culture and values at the forefront of analysis or study regarding occurrences and behaviors pertaining to the African diaspora. Understanding this perspective, in relation to the traditional American education system, helped to clarify many things for us as black college professors (especially as women) and our "place" within this firmly established system.

The traditional Eurocentric educational paradigm of objectivity presents a burden for the black educator to leave both cultural and spiritual identity at the door. The cultural norms of Afrocentricity adhere to a worldview in which spirituality is the central core of life, particularly as a means of resiliency to societal oppression: "Such spiritual centeredness rests within the person, and as such, has long been invoked by [Black] women" in their occupation or "calling" as "public school teachers and university professors" (Dillard, Abdur-Rashid, and Tyson, 2000, p. 449). It is interesting to note that earlier literature, reflecting on the educational experience of segregated schools, explained that black women teachers who taught black children with heart and spiritual inspiration were on a "mission." They were committed to a "liberatory cause, a spiritual purpose that permeated every act of thinking, being, and feeling" within the classroom (p. 450).

Patreece writes:

> As an instructor of intercultural and introductory communication courses, one of the core tenets that I teach students is that both consciously and subconsciously, they bring to the classroom their racial, religious, gendered, and social class identities, etc. I emphasize that such concepts are inescapable, and encourage my students to acknowledge and embrace these varied aspects

NEW DIRECTIONS FOR TEACHING AND LEARNING • DOI: 10.1002/tl

of their character or persona. Yet, while I often welcome and recognize the influence of my race, gender, and social class standpoints in classroom interactions, I am at times cautious in doing the same with my own spiritual beliefs; thereby, reflecting the position mentioned earlier by Dillard et al. (2000) whereby educators are often influenced to leave religious traditions and spirituality outside classroom doors.

Adapting to the context of a predominantly white university, which generally espouses a traditional Eurocentric educational philosophy of objectivity encouraging the separation of church and state, required a "shifting" (Jones & Shorter-Gooden, 2003) or identity modification on my part. As a result, I find myself restraining my spiritual self in classroom interactions, thus sometimes contributing to an internal conflict regarding how to best negotiate spiritual identity and purpose, a common struggle among working women of faith.

For example, when in the classroom, I do not hesitate to note how my Southern background (regional identity), my life as a woman and person of color (gender and racial identity), as well as my middle class status (social class identity) influence my perception of my surroundings as well as my perspective on various topics and current issues. In fact, not only do I embrace these aspects of my identity in the classroom, but I view them as essential in contributing to classroom dynamics. However, I feel that to draw attention to my Christian beliefs and faith (spiritual identity) somehow, on some level, discredits me as a college professor—an affliction in academe. No longer am I a knowledgeable, informed instructor, but I am crossing an invisible border between being offensive to some and violating another's constitutional rights. As a result, I struggle with the notion of freely acknowledging and embracing this aspect of my identity in the classroom. I can't help but question and wonder, "Am I implementing a self-imposed censoring of my spiritual self? And isn't the spiritual self the most significant aspect of my identity and who I claim to be?"

Similarly, I must also acknowledge the educational context in which I did not feel compelled to "shift" (Jones & Shorter-Gooden, 2003) or restrain the free expression of my spiritual self. Many years ago, when I taught at a small HBCU, I never paused to question the presence or acceptance of spiritual identities (both mine and my students) within the college classroom. Perhaps this is due to the fact that as African Americans, we shared cultural beliefs historically rooted in the Traditional African Worldview—a philosophy emphasizing humankind's relationship to God as the apex of the spiritual world (Daniel & Smitherman, 1990; Neuliep, 1995). Henceforth, when references to God or spiritual beliefs were made in the classroom (through expressions such as "thank you Jesus," "the Lord spoke to me"), such remarks were not questioned by me or the students. When I did reference my spirituality within the classroom, I did not fear my credibility would be questioned. Thus, I didn't face the internal turmoil concerning the spiritual influence on my overall effectiveness as an academic woman of faith.

Considine (2008), examining the tensions women face in combining faith and work, wrote in concluding remarks that "the move toward accepting spirituality at work appears not to have had any impact upon the workplaces of these women and the masculine, individualistic discourses still prevail in the workplace making the integration of womanhood, faith and work incredibly challenging" (pp. 22–23). Though it is often challenging to be a woman of faith within the realm of higher education, we hold fast to the concept that spirituality is a holistic concept, which cannot be separated from an educator who is rooted in and embraces an Afrocentric worldview. Belgrave and Allison (2006) explain that "spirituality is not separated from other aspects of one's life in African culture," but it is "woven into one's daily activities" (p. 35).

Spiritualized Pedagogy

Spirituality critically affects our pedagogical philosophy and our communicative practices. It is evidenced through our assignments, conferences with students, and cultural speech practices in the classroom. As faculty members at private and public predominantly white institutions (PWIs) in the Midwest and South, we are responsible for many typical faculty duties, including advising students, serving on university and departmental committees, and being faculty advisors for student organizations and graduate teaching assistants. However, spiritualized pedagogy remains at the foundation of our responsibilities. Belgrave and Allison (2006) explain that the "presence of spiritual beliefs is linked to positive and adaptive coping strategies like planning and organization" (p. 195). Additionally, a spiritual mindset that God is in control does not exempt us from accountability.

Audrey writes:

In the classroom, I advocate an organizing maxim of "plan your work and then work your plan." Although some of my students humorously note that they have never been asked to adopt a course motto, many embrace it and apply it to their personal lives. When mentoring individual students about career paths, graduate school, or other life-changing goals, I emphasize the importance of planning according to one's spiritual values. As a professor, it's great to hear my students' testimonies of being victorious through a struggle. Their success and appreciation causes my spirit to rejoice.

However, there are also times when a plan fails, a coveted opportunity slips by, and troubles mount, that I often hear the familiar "voices" of students, expressing frustration about difficult exams, internships, long campus commutes, and family pressure. While an objective, logistical response is often expected or warranted, I also sense that these same "voices" (revealing wearied or unnurtured spirits) are yearning for compassion, support, and inspiration. My intent is not to preach or judge, but rather to help my students feel restored and self-directed by their own spiritual core. Seeking to encourage my students, I ask them to ask themselves, "How might my own spirit empower me right now?" I challenge them to "rise, adapt, and overcome," reminding them that "troubles don't last always." It is my calling as an educator that requires me to teach and mentor this way, with spiritual accountability. As a Christian, I believe in the spiritual use of words to speak life into situations and quicken the soul to stand strong amid adversity. I mentor students to encourage themselves, to propel forward and "press toward the mark."

With regard to communication style, Dillard and colleagues (2000) argue that "both the overt invocation of spiritual language" and the subtle use of "spiritual concepts inform and guide Black women educators" (p. 449). Spiritualized pedagogy welcomes the souls of students into the classroom. Kessler (1998–99) explains that "when soul is present in education, we listen with great care not only to what is spoken but also to the messages between the words" (p. 50). The communication strategies implemented by African American educators also lead us to address a pertinent question regarding spirituality and teaching style. In their ethnographic study, Dillard and colleagues (2000) pose the question, "What does being a 'spiritual people' mean for the way African American educators 'educate'?" (p. 449). Although we feel there are potentially numerous responses to this question, this discussion highlights the connection between spiritual philosophy and communication style as critical influences.

Mattis's research (2002) on communicative strategies by which African American women acquired and validated knowledge reflects how spirituality is communicated in the classroom via black speech practices: visions, proverbs, metaphors, and double meanings. Previous research reveals that call and response, a black English speech pattern with distinct origins within black gospel oratory, can be used as an effective pedagogical and cultural tool between an African American professor and her students (Boone, 2003). Other research studies exploring black speech styles and performances (whose origins are of a spiritual nature) substantiate the effectiveness and positive impact of communicative strategies implemented by African American women educators on their students (Hollins, 1982; Foster, 1995).

Synthesis

On the basis of a reflective analysis of our own journey from doctoral students to university professors, the efficacy of spiritualized pedagogy, and comparable findings in the literature, we contend that spirituality, purpose, and cultural identity are critically intertwined. It is our cultural identity that enables us to define ourselves and navigate our place within our world and society. As spiritually motivated professors, we believe Afrocentricity is seemingly inseparable from our spiritual focus.

As a former student and educator within the context of an HBCU, Patreece found that the concept of spirituality was not questioned but in fact embraced, often serving as a cultural identity marker between African

American instructors and students. Audrey notes that the reference to common themes in African American society, including the black gospel church experience—emphasizing emotional and spiritual release—does not separate the person from the spirit but views the spirit as essential to one's existence and survival, both inside and outside academe.

Conclusion

According to Belgrave and Allison (2006), "worldview is a way of thinking that organizes all aspects of one's life, including intra- and interpersonal thoughts and behaviors and one's functioning in social systems and institutions in the community . . . and in larger society" (p. 27). The authors further state that "Spirituality exists across all socio-economic levels, age-groups, and geographical locations" (p. 35). As black educators, we find spirituality a significant foundation of our worldview, and a motivational force behind our present course in higher education. Before we began this research, we "understood" that our spiritual beliefs and foundation were significant to our individual and collective journey as students and then professors. However, we now realize that we have only scratched the surface of exploring and comprehending spirituality and its role in academia. Though often linked solely to religious practices, we adhere to the fundamental belief that spirituality is a core aspect of identity, defining our thought patterns and behaviors. Just as we cannot ignore the impact that our gendered and racial selves (for example) have on our classroom presence, we cannot separate or divide ourselves from our spiritual self and its impact. However, the drive to suppress the spiritual nature in the classroom often places university professors in a balancing act. For example, if we now live in a society that encourages us to proudly proclaim our racial, social class, age, and sexual orientation identities, why should we then stifle our spiritual identity, if it is the key to our "called" purpose and desire to educate? We therefore encourage others to ponder this question as well.

Lastly, we hope that this glimpse into "who we are" as spiritually motivated, academic women of color encourages others who are considering graduate education or are questioning their current journey. We suggest: look inward to your spirituality. Great mentors, advisors, cooperative committee members, fellow graduate students, and supportive colleagues are not always present for inspiration. Beliefs, however, rooted in a spiritual foundation are often all that one can rely on. Thus far, we have been quite intrigued and satisfied with our journey in academe. We continue to look forward to more professional and personal challenges, allowing our spirit to motivate us and light the path.

References

Asante, M. K. *The Afrocentric Idea.* Philadelphia: Temple University Press, 1987.

Asante, M. K. "The Afrocentric Idea in Education." *Journal of Negro Education*, 1991, *60*, 170–180.

Belgrave, F. Z., and Allison, K. W. *African American Psychology: From Africa to America.* Thousand Oaks, Calif.: Sage, 2006.

Boone, P. R. "When the "Amen Corner" Comes to Class: An Examination of Pedagogical and Cultural Impact of Call and Response Communication in the Black College Classroom." *Communication Education*, 2003, *52*, 212–229.

Considine, J. "Conflicted Identities: A Narrative Analysis of the Tensions Women Face in Combining Faith and Work." Paper presented to the International Communication Association, May 25, 2008, New York.

Daniel, J. L., and Smitherman, G. "How I Got Over: Communication Dynamics in the Black Community." In D. Carbaugh (ed.), *Cultural Communication and Intercultural Contact.* Hillsdale, N.J.: Erlbaum, 1990.

Delbecq, A. L. "How the Religious Traditions of Calling and Spiritual Friendship Shaped My Life as a Teacher/Scholar." *Management Communication Quarterly*, 2004, *17*, 621–627.

Dillard, C. B., Abdur-Rashid, D., and Tyson, C. A. "My Soul Is a Witness: Affirming Pedagogies of the Spirit." *International Journal of Qualitative Studies in Education*, 2000, *13*(5), 447–462.

Foster, M. "Talking That Talk: The Language of Control, Curriculum, and Critique." *Linguistics and Education*, 1995, *7*, 129–150.

Hollins, E. R. "The Marva Collins Story Revisited: Implications for Regular Classroom Instruction." *Journal of Teacher Education*, 1982, *33*, 37–40.

Jones, C., and Shorter-Gooden, K. *Shifting: The Double Lives of Black Women in America.* New York: HarperCollins, 2003.

Kessler, R. "Nourishing Students in Secular Schools." *Educational Leadership*, 1998–99, *56*(4), 49–52.

Lauzon, A. "The Challenges of Spirituality in the Everyday Practice of the Adult Educator." *Adult Learning*, 2001, *12*(3), 4.

Mattis, J. S. "Religion and Spirituality in the Meaning-Making and Coping Experiences of African American Women: A Qualitative Analysis." *Psychology of Women Quarterly*, 2002, *26*(4), 309–321.

Neuliep, J. W. "A Comparison of Teacher Immediacy in African-American and Euro-American College Classrooms." *Communication Education*, 1995, *44*, 267–277.

Oladele, F. "Passing Down the Spirit." *Educational Leadership*, 1998–99, *56*(4), 62–65.

Scott, K. D. "Crossing Cultural Borders: 'Girl' and 'Look' as Markers of Identity in Black Women's Language Use." In R. L. Jackson (ed.), *African American Communication and Identities: Essential Readings.* Thousand Oaks, Calif.: Sage, 2004.

Steingard, D. S. "The Spiritually Whole-System Classroom: A Transformational Application of Spirituality." *World Futures*, 2005, *61*, 228–246.

AUDREY M. WILSON ALLISON teaches courses in organizational communication at Kennesaw State University. Her research includes institutional images in higher education, organizational diversity, and service learning.

PATREECE R. BOONE BROADUS conducts research in intercultural communication, specifically black speech practices within the college classroom. She has taught courses in intercultural, nonverbal, interviewing, and human communication.

10

A Chinese American female professor discusses her teaching challenges and how her Christian faith influenced the educational methods she created to have students introspectively look within their humanness and spirituality as part of their assignments. Her approach to spiritual mentorship is also addressed.

The Spirit Moves Where There Is a Need in Higher Education

Mary Fong

A caption on the front page of today's Sunday local newspaper reads, "Grad Rate in Dire State" and "SB School District at Bottom of the List." I began reading the article and took note of some highlights:

> In the Manhattan Institute's recently released report that examined the nation's 100 largest urban school districts, the San Bernardino City Unified School District came in last at 42 percent [graduation rate]. The national average was 70 percent. . . . In the San Bernardino district, . . . slightly more than four in 10 students are graduating from the school district, the worst rate in the United States for large urban areas, a national study has found [*Grad Rate*, 2006, p. 1, A8].

The article cites extreme poverty, high mobility among families, and multiple families living in one house as characterizing the demographics existing in the district. Also, a high percentage of students at the university in the City of San Bernardino (CSB) are first-generation college-bound. The student population is diverse, and the university is designated as a Hispanic-serving institution.

I arrived at this university sixteen years ago as an assistant professor with an ABD (all but dissertation) for my first full-time teaching position. I had taught part-time at nine other Southern California universities and community colleges for almost four years prior to my doctoral studies. As a native Southern Californian, I had a perception that the CSB was a remote

NEW DIRECTIONS FOR TEACHING AND LEARNING, no. 120, Winter 2009   © Wiley Periodicals, Inc.
Published online in Wiley InterScience (www.interscience.wiley.com) • DOI: 10.1002/tl.380

area about sixty miles northeast of Los Angeles. The north end of the City of San Bernardino was relatively undeveloped. Some of the existing homes were run-down and did not have sidewalks. There were blocks and blocks of homes with nice lawns, but there were also miles and miles of empty dirt-filled land backed up against the foothills of the San Bernardino Mountains. Radio reception was poor, and the only stations I could get were country music. Not my cup of tea. I was the only Asian American female professor in the College of Arts and Letters for a few years. I felt isolated, and friendships were few.

It was rough, at times, in the first three years of teaching in CSB. Noticeably in the intercultural communication courses that I taught, some of the students were mean and rude to me. On the first day of classes, I instantly felt negative energy from a returning student who sat in the front row. Before I said one word, she immediately crossed both her hands and legs and looked directly out the window throughout the class period. As the weeks went on, negative energies from more students became apparent. A young Italian American student said to me at the beginning of class, "You just don't understand us. You just don't understand us!" I said, "What is it that you think I don't understand?" She repeated herself, "You just don't understand us. You just don't understand us!" and sat down at her seat. Another student made a comment after receiving the first assignment handout, "This looks like a stupid assignment!" I looked at her and then ignored her. Throughout the quarter I would catch glimpses of another female, a divorced student in her forties, giving dissatisfied looks. Am I in the middle of a nightmare? I knew that I was in for a spiritual challenge with some students.

A spiritual challenge for me involves a struggle within, where there exists a tension between doing "good" or what is "right," rather than succumbing to doing unfavorable acts or resorting to a sinful nature. Blackaby and Blackaby (2004) state that the Holy Spirit tries to keep a person from sin. Bynum (2002) also explains that when we surrender our hearts to God, He will do battle on our behalf.

The goal behind the spiritual challenge is to overcome an unfavorable situation or condition that tests a person to achieve a refined spirit that is aligned with one's Holy Spirit. Stanley (2002) explains, "The Holy Spirit gives a 'heart sense' to a person so that the person has an ability to recognize truth from lie, fact from fiction, right from wrong" (p. 23). He further elaborates, "The person who walks in Godly wisdom has a 'sense' or intuition provided by the Holy Spirit, who lives inside of every believer" (p. 23). A person is challenged to develop and keep strong the fruits of the Spirit that is love, joy, peace, patience, kindness, goodness, faithfulness, gentleness and self-control (Gal. 5:22, New International Version, the scriptural source used in all instances).

In this autoethnography, I share some of my experiences and how my spirituality informs me in the educational context with both students and faculty. I discuss spiritual challenges and my pedagogical approach toward the students I have encountered in my initial years as an assistant professor. After that, I discuss the importance of my mentorship style.

New Directions for Teaching and Learning • DOI: 10.1002/tl

To better understand how my spirituality informs me in my teaching and interactions at an institution of higher education, I will briefly talk about pertinent aspects of my background. I am second-generation Chinese American, raised in Southern California in various areas such as Long Beach, Torrance, Sun Valley, Chinatown, and Highland Park. My parents emigrated from Canton, China, in the late 1940s and mid-1950s. I have been a born-again Christian since the fifth grade but was not spiritually nourished. It was not until high school that I found a church where I understood better about God's love as it is discussed in Corinthians chapter 13. Two years later, I strayed from church when I started working on Sundays. It was not until 1992, nine months prior to starting my first tenure-track assistant professorship in Southern California, that I became a serious Christian. Beginning in this period, I learned a great deal from a gospel radio station. In 1994 I found a church to attend regularly and became an active member by teaching Sunday school, vacation bible school, and counseling at stadium-filled crusades. With this background, I incorporated aspects of spirituality into my college teaching in hope of bettering my students' educational and spiritual experiences.

A Spiritual Pedagogical Approach

When there are student problems and needs in my courses, I assess the situation and try to find ways to resolve them. The hostile students in my first quarter Intercultural Communication course emitted negativity through their verbal and nonverbal communications. My spirit was challenged, especially as a young faculty member. Fortunately, I had a handful of students who respected me. I believed that the negative students had judged and stereotyped me. They saw me as a new professor who was an outsider, that is, an outsider who was not from their inland region and not fitting the professorial image of a middle-class older Caucasian American male or female. I was surprised at the students' blatant negative verbal and nonverbal behaviors because I have never experienced this in my previous years of teaching. However, I did not feel that my ego was hurt by the students' negative energy toward me. By nature I am typically a calm and patient person, and I maintained this disposition throughout the entire quarter. My attitude was to do the best job I could and not to strive for perfection.

My spirituality guides me in how I conduct myself and what I want students to also follow. For example, treatment of others is a strong spiritual value to me. The bible teaches doing good to all (Gal. 6:10), having love for both your neighbors and your enemies (Matt. 5:43), showing respect to everyone (1 Peter 2:17), demonstrating brotherly kindness (2 Peter 1:5–7), and being considerate, impartial, and sincere (James 3:17).

In the seventh week of class in the first quarter, I was chatting with one student informally at the front of the classroom while a couple of remaining groups continued to discuss their project. I made it a point to speak loudly enough so that the negative students heard about my growing up in the Los Angeles area, working thirty hours a week, six days a week as an undergraduate, and taking the bus. The young Italian American student who said, "You just don't understand us" overheard my conversation; I felt that she had stereotyped me as a young Asian who sailed through school and came from a comfortable upbringing.

I found that in the first three years of teaching as an assistant professor, there were students who were ill-mannered. I felt that the culture of students in this region needed character education, meaning development and improvement of ethics, morals, and the spiritual qualities of a person. I theorized that in the educational context it is the praxis of spiritual communication in course design of assignments, reflection papers, videos, assignment of books, speaking activities, class discussions, and the mentorship of colleagues that offers a learning ambience that brings forth spiritual growth of participants. The spiritual challenge to them in their assignments takes them on a meaningful and introspective spiritual journey that is long-lasting and immeasurable in influence by way of their spiritual communicative praxis in their interactions with others.

The spring quarter when I taught Intercultural Communication, I assigned a book called *Celebrate Yourself*, by Dorothy Briggs (1986). This book engaged students to examine themselves as a person and to develop their self-esteem. They were required to write a paper reflecting on their behavior, thought patterns, and where they need to improve. In my Theories of Communication course, I had students read a supplement book called *Finding the Love of Your Life*, by Neil Warren (1992). He is a marriage and family psychologist and the founder of e-harmony, an Internet relationship matching service. Students are asked to incorporate Warren's concepts and theories and apply them to their personal experiences while writing in their journal. Both book assignments focused on the spiritual qualities of the person, educating the person and having students reflect on their being.

The Power of Shared Lived Experience. What I find spiritually powerful are the shared narrative experiences exchanged between the students and me in both oral and written form in several of my classes, as in Public Speaking, Intercultural Communication, Ethnography of Communication, and Culture and Ethnicity in Language. In the Public Speaking course, I have an activity called the Learning Experience. Both the students and I tell a personal narrative that reveals what we learned from the experience. I have heard very touching stories, such as a Vietnamese student and his family who escaped from Vietnam by boat. His family had made a first attempt in which they got caught and were imprisoned in a jail in which they only had space to stand. On the second attempt, the family missed the departure time. The father had planned for months and was very disheartened that they had mixed up the time of departure. A few weeks later, he came across a man who was supposed to have departed on the boat in the second attempt. The man said, "Did you not hear? I was the only survivor of that

NEW DIRECTIONS FOR TEACHING AND LEARNING • DOI: 10.1002/tl

boat, which exploded." The father was in shock and realized that he and his family would have died. In the final attempt, the father and his family made it through the choppy waters to eventually reach America. What the student learned was to never take anything for granted, realize that events happen for a reason, and, given the opportunity, to have freedom means to become all you can be. Students in class are able to comment and ask questions of each speaker.

In my upper-division culture courses, students have written and presented outstanding autoethnographies involving personal narratives of alcoholism, identity crisis, mistreatment, intercultural interactions, immigrant struggles crossing the border, a Japanese international student feeling alienated because her complexion was not fair enough, and so on. Both professor and students share personal narratives that create a positive synergy among everyone in class who experiences the life spirit. Synergy involves participants approaching each other in such a way that the scope of what they can achieve together far surpasses the total of what they could achieve separately (Wing, 1979). At times the speaker or the listeners shed tears because their spirits in the human form are experiencing this synergy of a heartfelt connection of understanding, triumph, despair, compassion, and so on. Through the sharing of narratives, everyone in the classroom is no longer a stranger, and no longer just a name or voice to a face. Instead there is something deeper: a person with a spirit. The sharing of one's spirit through personal narratives brings people together, creating a synergetic bond through significant and meaningful experiences that capture their essence.

Some of my published work and what I disclose in class humanize who I am to my students when a sharing of my personal narratives occurs. My position of power still exists, but a sharing of my personal narratives helps students to understand how communication theories and concepts function in everyday interaction. Moreover, I believe my storytelling experiences allow students to see me as a person who they can identify with in terms of everyday living that includes difficulties and problem solving of communication issues. The use of personal narratives I believe breaks down initial students' perception of the 'authority' or 'professorial' image which allows students to be open and receptive to me; and in turn that they will reciprocate in sharing their own personal narratives. My role as a college professor is profound. It is not just a career. I take my duties as a serious social responsibility to not only educate students in academics but to assist them in their development as a person, as a spirit that is having a human experience, a person who looks beyond self to contribute to society. My social responsibility as an educator and as a person stems from many biblical passages in influencing and developing a person's spirit. The Bible speaks of clothing "yourselves with compassion, kindness, humility, gentleness and patience. Bear with each other and forgive whatever grievances you may have against one another. Forgive as the Lord forgave you" (Col. 3:12–13, NIV pp. 1816–1817). The value of serving and contributing to society stems from a sample of bible verses: "to love the Lord your God and to serve Him with all your heart and with all your soul" (Deut. 11:13, p. 259), and to "not use your freedom to indulge the sinful nature, rather serve one another in love" (Gal. 5:13, p. 1787). The entire law is summed up in this command: "Love your neighbor as yourself" (Gal. 5:14, p. 1787). The significance of my role is my belief that we are here on earth to refine our spirits to be in alignment with God and to work against evil so that God's goodness will reign, rather than evil ruling to destroy and making the world chaotic, vicious, and ugly.

Mediated Learning Tool. The use of media in classroom learning is valuable to student learning and bringing forth spiritual discussions. A successful assignment in using films and videos involves writing a reflection paper by discussing academic concepts, illustrating these concepts as they function in the media. Moreover, the students discuss how the media events relate to them and what choices would they make and why. Students write about their communications within their lives and how they feel, think, and act in regard to the topic at hand (which might be feng shui, racism, white privilege, class, and so forth). Dee Fink (2003) states, "College students frequently report that learning about themselves and about others is among the most significant experiences they have during college" (p. 44).

These activities and assignments encourage the students to look introspectively at themselves as persons, as well as communicators and how they relate to others. Fink (2003) presents a taxonomy of significant learning experiences consisting of six dimensions in helping teachers in their course design. The human dimension is one of the significant learning experiences that address important relationships and interactions we have with one another. Fink explains, "When we learn how to fulfill these relationships in positive ways and how to honor and advance those relationships we learn something very important" (p. 44). Through these assignments, students are given the opportunity to explore and critically look at who they are and how they treat themselves and others. Listening to a multitude of life experiences encourages students' sensitivity, their perspectives of others, and hopefully compassion for their fellow beings.

Spiritually, I feel more connected to my students, knowing them better as people with their own unique experiences and trials in their lives. I feel that there is a shared honesty, realness, and heartfelt realizations that make what we do meaningful and purposeful for the good of our spirit. I feel that I have grown spiritually in terms of my purpose in serving God and His people and to act on every opportunity that I am given to fulfill my social responsibility toward the surrounding communities. At times there are opportunities in which I mentor both students and faculty regarding a variety of needs, concerns, and problems that may arise.

Mentoring

Mentoring is known to be the most effective method for helping young people increase their self-esteem and achieve their potential (Lasley, 1996). *Mentor* is defined as a person who serves as a guide who looks after, advises, protects, and takes a special interest in another's development (Sands, Parson, and Duane, 1991). Buell (2004) found four models of mentorship: cloning, nurturing, friendship, and apprenticeship. I have mentored undergraduates, graduate students, graduate teaching associates, part-time faculty, and tenure-track faculty.

Mentorship and Spirituality

My spirituality guides me in my mentoring relationship with my students and colleagues to be helpful, fair, compassionate, honest, and "self-emptying for others." Nouwen, McNeill, and Morrison (1982) discuss the compassion act of self-emptying for others,

> which involves the process of paying attention to others with the desire to make them the center and to make their interests our own. . . . When someone listens to us with real concentration and expresses sincere care for our struggles and our pains, we feel that something very deep is happening to us. Slowly, fears melt away, tensions dissolve, anxieties retreat, and we discover that we carry within us something we can trust and offer as a gift to others. The simple experience of being valuable and important to someone else has a tremendous re-creative power" [p. 81].

A new part-time instructor, who was my former graduate teaching associate, sent me an e-mail attaching a classroom observation evaluation written by a full-time lecturer who has a master's degree; she was afraid she would get terminated because of the negative and argumentative nature of the evaluation she received. It created undue stress for the first-year part-time instructor, a single mom and a former outstanding graduate student who had received a certificate of excellence in teaching independent sections in public speaking. As a graduate student she received student evaluations on her teaching that had scores over the college mean (nearly all 3.8 to 4.0 on a scale of 4.0), and her classroom teaching that I have observed was positive. It was a shock for this new part-time lecturer to receive a very negative evaluation from a full-time lecturer who came to observe her classroom teaching.

When I read her attachment, with the classroom evaluation report by the full-time lecturer, I thought I had never seen a classroom observation with negative comments consistently throughout. Typically classroom observations are positive, so it was quite unusual to see a very negative report. The evaluation was demeaning, dogmatic, and argumentative. The evaluation report lacked nurturance, support, and fairness. I responded to her e-mail and said I would call her that evening. She was distraught, and I told her that she had an option to write a rebuttal for her file. A few days later, I talked with the part-time instructor; she was upset by her ninety-minute postvisit with the lecturer. The part-time instructor said the lecturer was argumentative, forceful, and arrogant. I provided suggestions and feedback on her rebuttal. The department chair and I reminded her that the positive teaching evidence in her file would outweigh the classroom evaluation report.

The self-emptying for others involved me focusing on her concerns and listen to what she had to say. She felt demoralized by the dogmatic, insensitive, and condescending comments of the full-time lecturer. I felt the pain, injustice, and victimization she had suffered. I offered her comfort, support, and guidance to present her case. She felt immensely better and thanked me for giving her direction and support. Self-emptying for others is a spiritual gift of care, comfort, and guidance given to another being. The gift is genuine in that the process seeks no gains, rewards, or returns for self. It is a spiritual gift that money cannot buy but that the receiver deems significant and valuable.

Conclusion

Spiritualism can exist in a secular educational institution. I shared the spiritual challenge I had with students in my initial years of teaching as an assistant professor. I have discussed my spiritual pedagogical approach, which I integrate into my teaching strategies to touch the minds, hearts, and spirits of the students through reflection paper assignments, reading books touching on spirituality, having class discussions that allow sharing of students' experiences in relation to the academic matter, and videos that involve people challenging the human spirit in their daily lives.

Spiritualism can reign among faculty if we all work against unfairness, discrimination, favoritism, arrogance, lying, selfishness, power abuse, competition, jealousy, and undermining people. Politics support such behavior. Almost every university has people who have not yet learned to develop their spirituality. Instead they allow these unfavorable characteristics to drive their ego and ailment. People of this kind make the work environment unpleasant for all who are around.

A couple of years ago, I was sitting in church, and the pastor was talking about a small church in the San Bernardino mountains where the air is fresher and cleaner, surrounded by tall trees. He said he had a calling to go down from the mountain to the valley of the City of San Bernardino to start a church where there is a great need—poverty, single mothers, gangs, and crime. The minister said this was why he invested in building a million-dollar church by selling some of his land and real estate. Blackaby and Blackaby (2004) explain that God searches above all for one whose heart is pure and obedient: "When

NEW DIRECTIONS FOR TEACHING AND LEARNING • DOI: 10.1002/tl

He finds someone pure in heart, He'll fill that heart with His Spirit and move through that person's life with power" (p. 40).

As I sat in this beautiful large church, I was overwhelmed by the ambience and also the deep spiritual commitment of Pastor Jim and Debra Cobrae, who serve God by serving the people in need in the City of San Bernardino. I cried with the realization as to why I was teaching in the city of San Bernardino. I was guided here from God to do my part to serve the students and the people in need to make it a better place to live. I feel that my life in San Bernardino has come full circle, and I am grateful to help in any capacity. As Nouwen, McNeill, and Morrison (1982) have said, compassion is not just a feeling; it is an act of doing something for another who is in need.

References

Barker, K. *The NIV Study Bible*. Grand Rapids, Mich.: Zondervan, 1985.
Blackaby, H., and Blackaby, M. *What's So Spiritual About Your Gifts?* Springs: Multnomah, 2004.
Briggs, D. C. *Celebrate Yourself*. New York: Main Street Books, 1986.
Buell, C. "Models of Mentoring in Communication." *Communication Education*, 2004, 53(1), 56–73.
Bynum, J. *Matters of the Heart*. Lake Mary, Fla.: Charisma House, 2002.
Fink, L. D. *Creating Significant Learning Experiences*. San Francisco: Jossey-Bass, 2003.
Fisher, E. *Embraced by the Holy Spirit*. Shippensburg, Pa.: Destiny Image, 2005.
"Grad Rate in Dire State." *San Bernardino County Sun*, Apr. 30, 2006, pp. 1, A8.
Lasley, T. J. "On Mentoring: What Makes So Few So Special?" *Journal of Teacher Education*, 1996, 47, 307–309.
Nouwen, H., McNeill, D. P., and Morrison, D. A. *Compassion*. New York: Doubleday, 1982.
Sands, R. G., Parson, L. A., and Duane, J. "Faculty Mentoring Faculty in a Public University." *Journal of Higher Education*, 1991, 62, 174–193.
Stanley, C. *Walking Wisely*. Nashville, Tenn.: Nelson Books, 2002.
Warren, N. C. *Finding the Love of Your Life*. New York: Pocket Books, 1992.
Wing, R. L. *The I Ching Workbook*. Garden City, N.Y.: Doubleday, 1979.

MARY FONG is a full professor in the Communication Studies Department at the California State University, San Bernardino. Her areas of teaching and research are cultural and intercultural communication, ethnography of communication, spiritual communication, and instructional communication. She has published an intercultural communication textbook and authored numerous journal articles.

Epilogue

Katherine G. Hendrix, Janice D. Hamlet

In *As the Spirit Moves Us*, each contributor revealed the significance of spiritual guidance in fulfilling his or her academic duties. We sought to connect with our readers by employing the autoethnographic tradition of storytelling. We narrated personal stories, shifting between the inward gaze of autobiography and the outward gaze of ethnography. We used our voices to disclose our lived experience, including its more emotional, subjective dimensions. These reflective pieces revealed that (1) traditional research standpoints, including critical paradigms and perspectives regarding what constitutes legitimate knowledge, merit closer examination; and (2) a heightened sense of moral responsibility can be incorporated into our research methodology when our behavior is directed by the Spirit.

As evidenced in this volume, we are individuals connected by the responsibilities of a shared discipline, drawn together by our belief in the significance of teaching and managing with our entire being—spirit and all—rather than operating out of a superficial division of mind and soul. We have offered experiences seeking and abiding with the Spirit through meditation, prayer, hymnals, scripture, quotations, artifacts, journal entries, and communion with others as viable means of enhancing life in general, and more specifically our lives in academia. In the end, the contributors to this book are a group of imperfect, racially diverse women and men who have faith in the importance of garnering strength and direction from someone greater than themselves.

INDEX

persist in many STEM classrooms and laboratories. It is increasingly clear that major improvements to STEM under-graduate education require the interest and active engagement of key stakeholders, including STEM instructors, academic administrators, disciplinary societies, and government policymakers. This volume looks at the challenges of enhancing STEM education from the perspective of these different stakeholders. Each chapter provides an illumi-nating analysis of problems facing STEM education and suggests actions needed to strengthen STEM undergraduate education in a time when science and technology competence are more important than ever. The strategies advanced in this volume should be key elements of the coordinated, systemic effort necessary to implement lasting reform of STEM undergraduate education.
ISBN: 978-04704-97289

TL116   Team-Based Learning: Small-Group Learning's Next Big Step
         Larry K. Michaelsen, Michael Sweet, Dean X. Parmelee
         Team-Based Learning (TBL) is a unique form of small-group learning designed in and for the college classroom. TBL's special combination of incentives and corrective feedback quickly transforms groups into high-performance learning teams, with no time taken from the coverage of course content. In this issue of *New Directions for Teaching and Learning*, the authors describe the practical elements of TBL, how it can look in the classroom, and what they have learned as it has grown into an inter-disciplinary and international practice. Importantly, TBL is not about teaching but about learning. Several articles in this volume illustrate this emphasis by using TBL students' own words to reinforce key ideas.
         ISBN: 978-04704-62126

TL115   The Role of the Classroom in College Student Persistence
         John M. Braxton
         This issue of *New Directions for Teaching and Learning* brings into sharp focus the complex role college and university faculty play in shaping the persistence and departure decisions of undergraduate students. The authors review practices ranging from curricular structures and instructional staffing policies to faculty teaching methods, and they offer recommendations for many common problems. Taken together, the chapters outline the elements of a scholarship of practice centered on keeping students in school. College and university presidents, chief academic affairs officers, academic deans, directors and staff members of campus-based centers for teaching, and individuals responsible for enrollment management will find a great deal of practical wisdom in this volume.
         ISBN: 978-04704-22168

TL114   Information Literacy: One Key to Education
         Margit Misangyi Watts
         This issue draws on the expertise of librarians and faculty to highlight the central role of information literacy in higher education. The authors show how approaches to information literacy can be used to engage undergrad-uates in research and creative scholarship. The articles clarify definitions of information literacy and illustrate various means of curricular integration. Students regularly miss the relationship between the information-seeking process and the actual creation of knowledge. The authors in this issue support infusing the undergraduate curriculum with research-based learning to facilitate students' ability to define research for themselves. Most importantly, this volume argues, students' information literacy leads beyond finding information—it actually involves their creating knowledge. Education should focus on inquiry, research, and discovery as a frame of mind.

Our goal as educators should be to maintain and strengthen the *context* of learning while enhancing the *content* of a liberal education. This finally rests—as it always has—on a foundation of incorporating information literacy skills. Recent dramatic changes in the meaning of "information literacy" have left many educators scrambling to keep up. What has not changed is the importance of teaching students to find information that matters and then helping them figure out *why* it matters. These chapters can help us all integrate the new world of digital information into a relevant, timely approach to content and teaching practice.
ISBN: 978-04703-98715

TL113   **Educating Integrated Professionals: Theory and Practice on Preparation for the Professoriate**
Carol L. Colbeck, KerryAnn O'Meara, Ann E. Austin
This volume explores how to enhance doctoral education by preparing future faculty to integrate their work in two interrelated ways. The first mode encourages doctoral students—and their faculty mentors—to take advantage of the synergies among their teaching, research, and community service roles. The second mode of integration emphasizes connections between professional and academic aspects of faculty work. The authors draw on theories of identity development, professionalization, apprenticeship, socialization, mentoring, social networks, situated curriculum, concurrent curricula, and academic planning to illuminate some of the drawbacks of current education for the professoriate. They also point toward current programs and new possibilities for educating doctoral students who will be ready to begin their faculty careers as professionals who integrate teaching, research, and service.
ISBN: 978-04702-95403

TL112   **Curriculum Development in Higher Education: Faculty-Driven Processes and Practices**
Peter Wolf, Julia Christensen Hughes
Faculty within institutions of higher education are increasingly being asked to play leadership roles in curriculum assessment and reform initiatives. This change is being driven by quality concerns; burgeoning disciplinary knowledge; interest in a broader array of learning outcomes, including skills and values; and growing support for constructivist pedagogies and learning-centered, interdisciplinary curricula. It is essential that faculty be well prepared to take a scholarly approach to this work. To that end, this issue of *New Directions for Teaching and Learning* presents the frameworks used and lessons learned by faculty, administrators, and educational developers in a variety of curriculum assessment and development processes. Collectively, the authors in this volume present the context and catalysts of higher education curriculum reform, advocate for the Scholarship of Curriculum Practice (SoCP), provide examples of curricular assessment and development initiatives at a variety of institutional levels, suggest that educational developers can provide much support to such processes, and argue that this work has profound implications for the faculty role. Anyone involved in curriculum assessment and development will find food for thought in each chapter.
ISBN: 978-04702-78512

TL111   **Scholarship of Multicultural Teaching and Learning**
Matthew Kaplan, A.T. Miller
Because effective approaches to multicultural teaching and learning are still being developed in institutions across the U.S. and around the world, it is essential to study and document promising practices. It is only through rigorous research and comparative studies that we can be assured that the

significant investments many institutions are making in multicultural education for the development of individual student and faculty skills, and the overall betterment of society, will reap positive results. This volume of *New Directions for Teaching and Learning* provides the valuable results of such research as well as models for the types of research that others could carry out in this area. The volume will appeal to new and experienced practitioners of multicultural teaching. It offers documented illustrations of how such teaching is designed, carried out, and is effective in varied higher education contexts and in a wide range of disciplines representing the humanities, social sciences, engineering and math, and the arts.
ISBN: 978-04702-23826

TL110   Neither White Nor Male: Female Faculty of Color
Katherine Grace Hendrix
Given limited information on the academic experience in general and on the pedagogical strategies and strengths of faculty of color in particular, the scholars in this issue have come together to begin the process of articulating the academic experiences of female professors of color. While chronicling our challenges within academia as well as our contributions to the education of U.S. students, this collaborative effort will add depth to the existing literature on faculty of color, serve as a reference for positioning women of color within the larger context of higher education (moving us from the margin to the center), and lay a foundation for more inclusive future research.
ISBN: 04702-2382-6

TL109   Self-Authorship: Advancing Students' Intellectual Growth
Peggy S. Meszaros
This issue addresses the limitations of national efforts to focus students' intellectual development narrowly on testing and explores why educators in higher education should consider using the lens of self-authorship and the Learning Partnerships Model for a more holistic model of student intellectual development. The chapters provide examples of institutional transformations needed to support change in teaching and learning and examples of assessment, research, and curricular development based in self-authorship theory. The summary chapter by Marcia Baxter Magolda ties the themes from each of the chapters together and offers promise for the future. The final chapter provides ideas for next steps in promoting the use of self-authorship to advance the intellectual development of college students. The audience for this volume is broad, ranging from college faculty to student affairs faculty and staff to college administrators who are facing assessment challenges for reporting student learning outcomes to their various constituencies, agencies, and boards. This volume should also prove instructive to faculty embarking on curriculum revisions and identifying and measuring student learning outcomes for undergraduate and graduate students.
ISBN: 07879-9721-2

TL108   Developing Student Expertise and Community: Lessons from How People Learn
Anthony J. Petrosino, Taylor Martin, Vanessa Svihla
This issue presents research from a collaboration among learning scientists, assessment experts, technologists, and subject-matter experts, with the goal of producing adaptive expertise in students. The model is based on the National Research Council book *How People Learn*. The chapters present case studies of working together to develop learning environments centered on challenge-based instruction. While the strategies and research come from

engineering, they are applicable across disciplines to help students think about the process of problem solving.
ISBN: 07879-9574-6

TL107 **Exploring Research-Based Teaching**
Carolin Kreber
Investigates the wide scope research-based teaching, while focusing on two distinct forms. The first sees research-based teaching as student-focused, inquiry-based learning; students become generators of knowledge. The second perspective fixes the lens on teachers; the teaching is characterized by discipline-specific inquiry into the teaching process itself. Both methods have positive effects on student learning, and this volume explores research and case studies.
ISBN: 07879-9077-9

TL106 **Supplemental Instruction: New Visions for Empowering Student Learning**
Marion E. Stone, Glen Jacobs
Supplemental Instruction (SI) is an academic support model introduced over thirty years ago to help students be successful in difficult courses. SI teaches students how to learn via regularly scheduled, out-of-class collaborative sessions with other students. This volume both introduces the tenets of SI to beginners and brings those familiar up to speed with today's methods and the future directions. Includes case studies, how-to's, benefits to students and faculty, and more.
ISBN: 0-7879-8680-1

TL105 **A Laboratory for Public Scholarship and Democracy**
Rosa A. Eberly, Jeremy Cohen
Public scholarship has grown out of the scholarship-and-service model, but its end is democracy rather than volunteerism. The academy has intellectual and creative resources that can help build involved, democratic communities through public scholarship. Chapters present concepts, processes, and case studies from Penn State's experience with public scholarship.
ISBN: 0-7879-8530-9

TL104 **Spirituality in Higher Education**
Sherry L. Hoppe, Bruce W. Speck
With chapters by faculty and administrators, this book investigates the role of spirituality in educating the whole student while recognizing that how spirituality is viewed, taught, and experienced is intensely personal. The goal is not to prescribe a method for integrating spirituality but to offer options and perspectives. Readers will be reminded that the quest for truth and meaning, not the destination, is what is vitally important.
ISBN: 0-7879-8363-2

TL103 **Identity, Learning, and the Liberal Arts**
Ned Scott Laff
Argues that we must foster conversations between liberal studies and student development theory, because the skills inherent in liberal learning are the same skills used for personal development. Students need to experience core learning that truly influences their critical thinking skills, character development, and ethics. Educators need to design student learning encounters that develop these areas. This volume gives examples of how liberal arts education can be a healthy foundation for life skills.
ISBN: 0-7879-8333-0

TL102   **Advancing Faculty Learning Through Interdisciplinary Collaboration**
Elizabeth G. Creamer, Lisa R. Lattuca
Explores why stakeholders in higher education should refocus attention on collaboration as a form of faculty learning. Chapters give theoretical basis then practical case studies for collaboration's benefits in outreach, scholarship, and teaching. Also discusses impacts on education policy, faculty hiring and development, and assessment of collaborative work.
ISBN: 0-7879-8070-6

TL101   **Enhancing Learning with Laptops in the Classroom**
Linda B. Nilson, Barbara E. Weaver
This volume contains case studies—mostly from Clemson University's leading-edge laptop program—that address victories as well as glitches in teaching with laptop computers in the classroom. Disciplines using laptops include psychology, music, statistics, animal sciences, and humanities. The volume also advises faculty on making a laptop mandate successful at their university, with practical guidance for both pedagogy and student learning.
ISBN: 0-7879-8049-8

TL100   **Alternative Strategies for Evaluating Student Learning**
Michelle V. Achacoso, Marilla D. Svinicki
Teaching methods are adapting to the modern era, but innovation in assessment of student learning lags behind. This volume examines theory and practical examples of creative new methods of evaluation, including authentic testing, testing with multimedia, portfolios, group exams, visual synthesis, and performance-based testing. Also investigates improving students' ability to take and learn from tests, before and after.
ISBN: 0-7879-7970-8

TL99   **Addressing Faculty and Student Classroom Improprieties**
John M. Braxton, Alan E. Bayer
Covers the results of a large research study on occurrence and perceptions of classroom improprieties by both students and faculty. When classroom norms are violated, all parties in a classroom are affected, and teaching and learning suffer. The authors offer guidelines for both student and faculty classroom behavior and how institutions might implement those suggestions.
ISBN: 0-7879-7794-2

TL98   **Decoding the Disciplines: Helping Students Learn Disciplinary Ways of Thinking**
David Pace, Joan Middendorf
The Decoding the Disciplines model is a way to teach students the critical-thinking skills required to understand their specific discipline. Faculty define bottlenecks to learning, dissect the ways experts deal with the problematic issues, and invent ways to model experts' thinking for students. Chapters are written by faculty in diverse fields who successfully used these methods and became involved in the scholarship of teaching and learning.
ISBN: 0-7879-7789-6

TL97   **Building Faculty Learning Communities**
Milton D. Cox, Laurie Richlin
A very effective way to address institutional challenges is a faculty learning community. FLCs are useful for preparing future faculty, reinvigorating senior faculty, and implementing new courses, curricula, or campus initiatives. The results of FLCs parallel those of student learning communities, such as reten-tion, deeper learning, respect for others, and greater civic participation. This

volume describes FLCs from a practitioner's perspective, with plenty of advice, wisdom, and lessons for starting your own FLC.
ISBN: 0-7879-7568-0

TL96   Online Student Ratings of Instruction
        Trav D. Johnson, D. Lynn Sorenson
        Many institutions are adopting Web-based student ratings of instruction, or are considering doing it, because online systems have the potential to save time and money among other benefits. But they also present a number of challenges. The authors of this volume have firsthand experience with electronic ratings of instruction. They identify the advantages, consider costs and benefits, explain their solutions, and provide recommendations on how to facilitate online ratings.
        ISBN: 0-7879-7262-2

TL95   Problem-Based Learning in the Information Age
        Dave S. Knowlton, David C. Sharp
        Provides information about theories and practices associated with problem-based learning, a pedagogy that allows students to become more engaged in their own education by actively interpreting information. Today's professors are adopting problem-based learning across all disciplines to faciliate a broader, modern definition of what it means to learn. Authors provide practical experience about designing useful problems, creating conducive learning environments, facilitating students' activities, and assessing students' efforts at problem solving.
        ISBN: 0-7879-7172-3

TL94   Technology: Taking the Distance out of Learning
        Margit Misangyi Watts
        This volume addresses the possibilities and challenges of computer technology in higher education. The contributors examine the pressures to use technology, the reasons not to, the benefits of it, the feeling of being a learner as well as a teacher, the role of distance education, and the place of computers in the modern world. Rather than discussing only specific successes or failures, this issue addresses computers as a new cultural symbol and begins meaningful conversations about technology in general and how it affects education in particular.
        ISBN: 0-7879-6989-3

TL93   Valuing and Supporting Undergraduate Research
        Joyce Kinkead
        The authors gathered in this volume share a deep belief in the value of undergraduate research. Research helps students develop skills in problem solving, critical thinking, and communication, and undergraduate researchers' work can contribute to an institution's quest to further knowledge and help meet societal challenges. Chapters provide an overview of undergraduate research, explore programs at different types of institutions, and offer suggestions on how faculty members can find ways to work with undergraduate researchers.
        ISBN: 0-7879-6907-9

TL92   The Importance of Physical Space in Creating Supportive Learning Environments
        Nancy Van Note Chism, Deborah J. Bickford
        The lack of extensive dialogue on the importance of learning spaces in higher education environments prompted the essays in this volume. Chapter authors look at the topic of learning spaces from a variety of perspectives,

elaborating on the relationship between physical space and learning, arguing for an expanded notion of the concept of learning spaces and furnishings, talking about the context within which decision making for learning spaces takes place, and discussing promising approaches to the renovation of old learning spaces and the construction of new ones.
ISBN: 0-7879-6344-5

TL91 **Assessment Strategies for the On-Line Class: From Theory to Practice**
Rebecca S. Anderson, John F. Bauer, Bruce W. Speck
Addresses the kinds of questions that instructors need to ask themselves as they begin to move at least part of their students' work to an on-line format. Presents an initial overview of the need for evaluating students' on-line work with the same care that instructors give to the work in hard-copy format. Helps guide instructors who are considering using on-line learning in conjunction with their regular classes, as well as those interested in going totally on-line.
ISBN: 0-7879-6343-7

TL90 **Scholarship in the Postmodern Era: New Venues, New Values, New Visions**
Kenneth J. Zahorski
A little over a decade ago, Ernest Boyer's *Scholarship Reconsidered* burst upon the academic scene, igniting a robust national conversation that maintains its vitality to this day. This volume aims at advancing that important conversation. Its first section focuses on the new settings and circumstances in which the act of scholarship is being played out; its second identifies and explores the fresh set of values currently informing today's scholarly practices; and its third looks to the future of scholarship, identifying trends, causative factors, and potentialities that promise to shape scholars and their scholarship in the new millennium.
ISBN: 0-7879-6293-7

TL89 **Applying the Science of Learning to University Teaching and Beyond**
Diane F. Halpern, Milton D. Hakel
Seeks to build on empirically validated learning activities to enhance what and how much is learned and how well and how long it is remembered. Demonstrates that the movement for a real science of learning—the application of scientific principles to the study of learning—has taken hold both under the controlled conditions of the laboratory and in the messy real-world settings where most of us go about the business of teaching and learning.
ISBN: 0-7879-5791-7

TL88 **Fresh Approaches to the Evaluation of Teaching**
Christopher Knapper, Patricia Cranton
Describes a number of alternative approaches, including interpretive and critical evaluation, use of teaching portfolios and teaching awards, performance indicators and learning outcomes, technology-mediated evaluation systems, and the role of teacher accreditation and teaching scholarship in instructional evaluation.
ISBN: 0-7879-5789-5

TL87 **Techniques and Strategies for Interpreting Student Evaluations**
Karron G. Lewis
Focuses on all phases of the student rating process—from data-gathering methods to presentation of results. Topics include methods of encouraging meaningful evaluations, mid-semester feedback, uses of quality teams and

focus groups, and creating questions that target individual faculty needs and interest.
ISBN: 0-7879-5789-5

TL86   **Scholarship Revisited: Perspectives on the Scholarship of Teaching**
        Carolin Kreber
        Presents the outcomes of a Delphi Study conducted by an international panel of academics working in faculty evaluation scholarship and postsecondary teaching and learning. Identifies the important components of scholarship of teaching, defines its characteristics and outcomes, and explores its most pressing issues.
        ISBN: 0-7879-5447-0

TL85   **Beyond Teaching to Mentoring**
        Alice G. Reinarz, Eric R. White
        Offers guidelines to optimizing student learning through classroom activities as well as peer, faculty, and professional mentoring. Addresses mentoring techniques in technical training, undergraduate business, science, and liberal arts studies, health professions, international study, and interdisciplinary work.
        ISBN: 0-7879-5617-1

NEW DIRECTIONS FOR TEACHING AND LEARNING

ORDER FORM SUBSCRIPTION AND SINGLE ISSUES

DISCOUNTED BACK ISSUES:

Use this form to receive 20% off all back issues of *New Directions for Teaching and Learning*.
All single issues priced at **$23.20** (normally $29.00)

TITLE	ISSUE NO.	ISBN
_____	_____	_____
_____	_____	_____
_____	_____	_____

*Call 888-378-2537 or see mailing instructions below. When calling, mention the promotional code JBXND
to receive your discount. For a complete list of issues, please visit www.josseybass.com/go/ndtl*

SUBSCRIPTIONS: (1 YEAR, 4 ISSUES)

☐ New Order   ☐ Renewal

U.S.	☐ Individual: $89	☐ Institutional: $242
CANADA/MEXICO	☐ Individual: $89	☐ Institutional: $282
ALL OTHERS	☐ Individual: $113	☐ Institutional: $316

*Call 888-378-2537 or see mailing and pricing instructions below.
Online subscriptions are available at www.interscience.wiley.com*

ORDER TOTALS:

Issue / Subscription Amount: $ _____

Shipping Amount: $ _____
(for single issues only – subscription prices include shipping)

Total Amount: $ _____

SHIPPING CHARGES:

	SURFACE	DOMESTIC	CANADIAN
First Item		$5.00	$6.00
Each Add'l Item		$3.00	$1.50

*(No sales tax for U.S. subscriptions. Canadian residents, add GST for subscription orders. Individual rate subscriptions must
be paid by personal check or credit card. Individual rate subscriptions may not be resold as library copies.)*

BILLING & SHIPPING INFORMATION:

☐ **PAYMENT ENCLOSED:** *(U.S. check or money order only. All payments must be in U.S. dollars.)*

☐ **CREDIT CARD:** ☐ VISA ☐ MC ☐ AMEX

Card number _____ Exp. Date_____

Card Holder Name_____ Card Issue # *(required)* _____

Signature _____ Day Phone_____

☐ **BILL ME:** *(U.S. institutional orders only. Purchase order required.)*

Purchase order # _____
      Federal Tax ID 13559302 • GST 89102-8052

Name_____

Address_____

Phone_____ E-mail_____

Copy or detach page and send to: **John Wiley & Sons, PTSC, 5th Floor**
    989 Market Street, San Francisco, CA 94103-1741

Order Form can also be faxed to: **888-481-2665**

PROMO JBXND

NEW DIRECTIONS FOR TEACHING AND LEARNING IS NOW AVAILABLE ONLINE AT WILEY INTERSCIENCE

What is Wiley InterScience?

Wiley InterScience is the dynamic online content service from John Wiley & Sons delivering the full text of over 300 leading scientific, technical, medical, and professional journals, plus major reference works, the acclaimed Current Protocols laboratory manuals, and even the full text of select Wiley print books online.

What are some special features of Wiley InterScience?

Wiley Interscience Alerts is a service that delivers table of contents via e-mail for any journal available on Wiley InterScience as soon as a new issue is published online.
EarlyView is Wiley's exclusive service presenting individual articles online as soon as they are ready, even before the release of the compiled print issue. These articles are complete, peer-reviewed, and citable.
CrossRef is the innovative multi-publisher reference linking system enabling readers to move seamlessly from a reference in a journal article to the cited publication, typically located on a different server and published by a different publisher.

How can I access Wiley InterScience?

Visit http://www.interscience.wiley.com.

Guest Users can browse Wiley InterScience for unrestricted access to journal tables of contents and article abstracts, or use the powerful search engine.
Registered Users are provided with a *Personal Home Page* to store and manage customized alerts, searches, and links to favorite journals and articles. Additionally, Registered Users can view free online sample issues and preview selected material from major reference works.
Licensed Customers are entitled to access full-text journal articles in PDF, with select journals also offering full-text HTML.

How do I become an Authorized User?

Authorized Users are individuals authorized by a paying Customer to have access to the journals in Wiley InterScience. For example, a university that subscribes to Wiley journals is considered to be the Customer. Faculty, staff, and students authorized by the university to have access to those journals in Wiley InterScience are Authorized Users. Users should contact their library for information on which Wiley journals they have access to in Wiley InterScience.

ASK YOUR INSTITUTION ABOUT WILEY INTERSCIENCE TODAY!

UNITED STATES POSTAL SERVICE ® — Statement of Ownership, Management, and Circulation (All Periodicals Publications Except Requester Publications)

1. Publication Title	2. Publication Number	3. Filing Date
New Directions for Teaching and Learning	0 2 7 1 _ 0 6 3 3	10/1/2009

4. Issue Frequency	5. Number of Issues Published Annually	6. Annual Subscription Price
Quarterly	4	$89

7. Complete Mailing Address of Known Office of Publication *(Not printer)* *(Street, city, county, state, and ZIP+4®)*

Wiley Subscription Services, Inc. at Jossey-Bass, 989 Market St., San Francisco, CA 94103

Contact Person: Joe Schuman
Telephone *(Include area code)*: 415-782-3232

8. Complete Mailing Address of Headquarters or General Business Office of Publisher *(Not printer)*

Wiley Subscription Services, Inc., 111 River Street, Hoboken, NJ 07030

9. Full Names and Complete Mailing Addresses of Publisher, Editor, and Managing Editor *(Do not leave blank)*

Publisher *(Name and complete mailing address)*

Wiley Subscription Services, Inc., A Wiley Company at San Francisco, 989 Market St., San Francisco, CA 94103-1741

Editor *(Name and complete mailing address)*

Marilla D. Svinicki, Center for Teaching Effectiveness/University of Austin, Main Bldg., 2200 Austin, TX 78712-1111

Managing Editor *(Name and complete mailing address)*

None

10. Owner *(Do not leave blank. If the publication is owned by a corporation, give the name and address of the corporation immediately followed by the names and addresses of all stockholders owning or holding 1 percent or more of the total amount of stock. If not owned by a corporation, give the names and addresses of the individual owners. If owned by a partnership or other unincorporated firm, give its name and address as well as those of each individual owner. If the publication is published by a nonprofit organization, give its name and address.)*

Full Name	Complete Mailing Address
Wiley Subscription Services	111 River Street, Hoboken, NJ
(see attached list)	

11. Known Bondholders, Mortgagees, and Other Security Holders Owning or Holding 1 Percent or More of Total Amount of Bonds, Mortgages, or Other Securities. If none, check box ➤ ☑ None

Full Name	Complete Mailing Address

12. Tax Status *(For completion by nonprofit organizations authorized to mail at nonprofit rates) (Check one)*
The purpose, function, and nonprofit status of this organization and the exempt status for federal income tax purposes:
☐ Has Not Changed During Preceding 12 Months
☐ Has Changed During Preceding 12 Months *(Publisher must submit explanation of change with this statement)*

13. Publication Title	14. Issue Date for Circulation Data Below
New Directions for Teaching and Learning	Summer 2009

15. Extent and Nature of Circulation

			Average No. Copies Each Issue During Preceding 12 Months	No. Copies of Single Issue Published Nearest to Filing Date
a. Total Number of Copies (Net press run)			1272	1294
b. Paid Circulation (By Mail and Outside the Mail)	(1)	Mailed Outside-County Paid Subscriptions Stated on PS Form 3541 (Include paid distribution above nominal rate, advertiser's proof copies, and exchange copies)	558	535
	(2)	Mailed In-County Paid Subscriptions Stated on PS Form 3541 (Include paid distribution above nominal rate, advertiser's proof copies, and exchange copies)	0	0
	(3)	Paid Distribution Outside the Mails Including Sales Through Dealers and Carriers, Street Vendors, Counter Sales, and Other Paid Distribution Outside USPS®	0	0
	(4)	Paid Distribution by Other Classes of Mail Through the USPS (e.g. First-Class Mail®)	0	0
c. Total Paid Distribution (Sum of 15b (1), (2), (3), and (4))			558	535
d. Free or Nominal Rate Distribution (By Mail and Outside the Mail)	(1)	Free or Nominal Rate Outside-County Copies included on PS Form 3541	8	9
	(2)	Free or Nominal Rate In-County Copies Included on PS Form 3541	0	0
	(3)	Free or Nominal Rate Copies Mailed at Other Classes Through the USPS (e.g. First-Class Mail)	0	0
	(4)	Free or Nominal Rate Distribution Outside the Mail (Carriers or other means)	0	0
e. Total Free or Nominal Rate Distribution (Sum of 15d (1), (2), (3) and (4))			8	9
f. Total Distribution (Sum of 15c and 15e) ➤			566	544
g. Copies not Distributed (See Instructions to Publishers #4 (page #3)) ➤			706	750
h. Total (Sum of 15f and g) ➤			1272	1294
i. Percent Paid (15c divided by 15f times 100) ➤			99%	98%

16. Publication of Statement of Ownership

☐ If the publication is a general publication, publication of this statement is required. Will be printed in the ___Winter 2009___ issue of this publication.

☐ Publication not required.

17. Signature and Title of Editor, Publisher, Business Manager, or Owner

Susan E. Lewis, VP & Publisher - Periodicals   *[signature: Susan Lewis]*   Date: 10/1/2009

I certify that all information furnished on this form is true and complete. I understand that anyone who furnishes false or misleading information on this form or who omits material or information requested on the form may be subject to criminal sanctions (including fines and imprisonment) and/or civil sanctions (including civil penalties).